GMAT Practice Questions

Problem Solving

GMAT Free
www.GMATFree.com

© Copyright 2014 GMAT Free, LLC, an operating name of Test Free, LLC, 1330 S Indiana Ave, Chicago, IL 60605

ISBN-13: 978-1501092107

ISBN-10: 1501092103

All rights reserved. No part of this book may be used or reproduced in any manner whatsoever without written permission of the copyright holder.

GMAT is a registered trademark of the Graduate Management Admission Council. Test Free, LLC materials do not contain official items and are neither endorsed by nor affiliated with GMAC.

Printed in the United States of America.

For information, contact us at www.gmatfree.com/contact-us/.

CONTENTS

Introduction 1
Problem Solving Strategy 2
Problem Solving Practice Questions 3
What's Next? 457
Index of Questions 458

INTRODUCTION

This volume includes practice in Problem Solving, one of the two question types on the Quantitative section of the GMAT.

Of all GMAT question types, Problem Solving questions (along with Reading Comprehension) most closely resemble questions on other standardized tests. They are, arguably, the most "typical" test questions. Meanwhile, they are intermingled throughout the Quantitative section with questions of the Data Sufficiency format – the question type most unique to the GMAT.

Since both Quantitative question types draw on the same required body of mathematics knowledge, a comfortable and thorough way to prepare for the Quant section is to drill Problem Solving questions initially and work Data Sufficiency questions into your practice as you become comfortable with the mathematics involved. If you are preparing for the GMAT in a short time window (two weeks or less), you should cut away from this volume and to Data Sufficiency questions as quickly as possible.

The questions in this volume are realistic simulations of official GMAT items. Each is benchmarked against a real GMAT question in its format, difficulty, subject matter, and concepts tested. Don't concern yourself with the difficulty of individual questions, since the difficulty of even a perfectly normed question is a statistical outcome of a group of test takers. One person's easy question may be another person's difficult question, and *vice versa*.

Your guide in this review is Andrew Mitchell, Chief Freedom Officer of GMAT Free LLC, the former Director of GMAT Programs at Kaplan Test Prep, dubbed the "Guru of the GMAT" by Poets & Quants, and cited as a GMAT expert by publications including *The Wall Street Journal*, *The New York Times* and *Bloomberg BusinessWeek*.

For additional resources and updates, join us online. GMAT Free offers a complete, free GMAT course at www.gmatfree.com.

Thank you for your purchase. Let's practice!

\>> Download the free
PS Strategy Sheets

GMATFree.com/PS-Strategy-Sheets

PROBLEM SOLVING STRATEGY

The strategic challenge of Problem Solving questions is that they are not universally solvable by a specific approach. The best strategy is to consider a variety of approaches when first encountering a question and choose the method that appears easiest. The primary Problem Solving methods are:

A. Exact method or formula. A specific method or formula does not exist for every question type, but if it does, it is often the most straightforward solution. Telltale signs that you can solve directly include:

- Linear or quadratic equations
- Radicals and exponents
- Geometry
- Odd/even number properties
- Speed and rates
- Combined rates of work
- Averages of a set of values
- Probabilities
- Simple and compound interest
- Absolute value equations and inequalities

In the course of doing these questions, we will review all the specific methods and formulas you need for the exam. For a standalone review of these topics, see also *GMAT Math* by GMAT Free.

B. Analysis by cases. Although most questions can be solved by exact methods, you should *always* consider whether you can solve a Problem Solving question by analyzing cases. Straightforward methods are often slower and sometimes entirely impractical. Examples of analysis by cases include:

- **Plugging in answer choices.** Simply testing answer choices can solve many questions swiftly.
- **"Typical" numbers.** A question may describe a situation in general terms. You can often make the question simple by picking a case that is allowed by the question and which is easy to work with. For example, if you know that you will have to divide an unspecified sum of money by 4 or by 6, you might imagine that the sum of money is $24, if such a case is allowed by the question. Or, if you are calculating a percent of an unknown quantity, you may be able to solve quickly by imagining that the quantity is 100.
- **"Unusual" numbers.** If you want to know whether a statement is *always* true or *must be* true, it's useful to study unusual cases, such as large positive numbers, negative numbers, fractional numbers, 0, 1, 2, and numbers between 0 and 1. For example, suppose that you wanted to know whether it was always true that $x^2 > x$. If you tested only positive numbers greater than 1, you might think, "yes," but testing $x = 0.5$ reveals that the statement is not true for all values of x.
- **Enumeration/exhaustive cases.** Sometimes a general condition can be listed out as specific cases. For example, if a question asks about "all multiples of 8 less than 100," one approach is to list all such multiples, evaluate each separately, and compile the results to answer the question. Another example is to study a variable by examining cases in which it's positive, negative, or zero.

C. Estimation and guessing are less exact, but sometimes lead quickly to an answer, and they can help to manage your overall timing on the Quantitative section.

PROBLEM SOLVING PRACTICE QUESTIONS

Each of two buses contains y passengers. Each passenger carries x folders, and each folder contains 10 pieces of paper. How many pieces of paper are contained within the two buses?

- $10xy$
- $\frac{10x}{y}$
- $20xy$
- $\frac{20x}{y}$
- $\frac{20}{xy}$

Buses, Passengers, and Folders

Each of two buses contains y passengers. Each passenger carries x folders, and each folder contains 10 pieces of paper. How many pieces of paper are contained within the two buses?

- $10xy$
- $\dfrac{10x}{y}$
- $20xy$
- $\dfrac{20x}{y}$
- $\dfrac{20}{xy}$

Explanation

This is a great first Problem Solving question, because, behind the algebra, we are dealing with a ratio, and ratios are one of the least-appreciated topic areas on the Quantitative section on the GMAT.

The key to ratios is to work with fractions and take careful note of units. We can do this, starting from the end of the question prompt. We are asked for pieces of paper. The proceeding sentence tells us that we have 10 pieces of paper per folder. "Per" can be thought of as a word that indicates the line of a fraction, so we can write:

$$\frac{10 \text{ papers}}{\text{folder}}$$

Similarly, we have $\dfrac{1 \text{ passenger}}{x \text{ folders}}$. We can multiply these fractions so that the units cancel.

$$\frac{10 \text{ papers}}{\text{folder}} \times \frac{x \text{ folders}}{\text{passenger}} = \frac{10x \text{ papers}}{\text{passenger}}.$$

Notice that if you write the fractions with the units included, it's much easier to make sure you don't have the fractions flipped from what they should be. Lastly, we multiply by the number of passengers:

$$\frac{10x \text{ papers}}{\text{passenger}} \times y \text{ passengers} = 10xy \text{ papers}$$

We're done, right? In this last step also, we can use units and watch them cancel on the top and bottom of the fraction to ensure that we are multiplying the right things. This method of using units is called (or is related to what is called) dimensional analysis by some scientists. It works well to stay organized and avoid error on both easier and more difficult GMAT questions involving ratios and/or different types of units.

As a final step, we can make sure that all the units are accounted for. And, as a matter of fact, there is a unit that's not apparent in our scratch work above: buses. We're not looking for papers per bus; we're looking for paper per *two* buses. So, for two buses, we have to multiply $10xy$ by 2 to obtain $20xy$. Writing and thinking in units helps to avoid overlooking this step. The correct answer is (C).

The sum of prime numbers that are greater than 50 but less than 60 is

- 59
- 112
- 167
- 169
- 220

Sum of Primes

The sum of prime numbers that are greater than 50 but less than 60 is

- 59
- 112
- 167
- 169
- 220

Explanation

The key to this question is that we are only talking about 9 numbers that are possibly prime. A formal mathematical approach would be quite difficult, but analysis by cases is easy if we know a few basic rules. There is a finite list of possibilities to consider, so we can start by considering each of these numbers and determining whether or not it's prime.

So, we will start with 51 and count up. The number 51 is divisible by 3, because its digits sum to 6, which is divisible by 3. Then, 52 is even, and the only even prime number is 2, so 52 is not a prime number. The number 53 might be prime. A sure way to test whether a number is prime is to start with a nearby perfect square. 53 is less than 64, which is 8^2. That means we can find out whether 53 is prime by checking all integers from 1 to 8. The reason is this works is that factors come in pairs, so if 53 had a factor above 8, it would be paired with a factor below 8. The number 2 isn't a factor of 53, because 53 is odd. The number 3 isn't a factor, because, the digits of 53 add up to 8, which is not divisible by 3. The number 4, 5, and 6 all also fail to go into 53. You can check each one either by doing long division, or by counting out multiples. For example, $4 \times 12 = 48$ and $4 \times 13 = 52$ and $4 \times 14 = 56$, so 4 is not a factor of 56. Similarly, 7 and 8 are not factors of 53 because they multiply to 56, which is only 3 away. Therefore, 53 is a prime number: its only factors are 1 and itself.

The next few numbers are not prime. Namely, 54 is even, 55 is divisible by 5, 56 is even. The number 57 has digits that sum to 12, which is divisible by 3, so 57 is divisible by 3. Then, 58 is even, so it's not prime. The number 59 might be prime. So for primes, we have 53 and maybe 59. Checking the answer choices, I see that 53 isn't an option, so 59 must be a prime (which we could have confirmed), and the correct answer is $53 + 59 = 112$, or (B).

No GMAT question will require you to have memorized primes, but you have to know how to identify whether a number is prime, using the method we just discussed. The method is not much harder for larger numbers. For example, say, on a different question, you want to determine whether the number 111 is prime. The closest perfect squares are $10^2 = 100$ and $11^2 = 121$, so to find out whether 111 is prime, we will have to check at most possible factors from 2 up to 10. As it turns out, in this case we will stop at 3. We can see that 111 is divisible by 3 either by performing long division or by seeing that the digits of 111 sum to a number that is divisible by 3 (in this case, they sum to 3).

Again, the correct answer is (B).

For which of the following values of k is $\frac{k+20}{k}$ NOT an integer?

- 1
- 2
- 3
- 4
- 5

Generating a Non-Integer

For which of the following values of k is $\frac{k+20}{k}$ NOT an integer?

- 1
- 2
- 3
- 4
- 5

Explanation

This question can be solved quickly by trying answer choices. We might as well start with 3, since it isn't a factor of 20 and will go in the denominator. Indeed, $\frac{23}{3}$ is $7\frac{2}{3}$, so it is not an integer.

The correct answer is (C).

A family had a goal to save $1,890 over the course of a year by making equal monthly deposits into a savings account. At the end of the fourth month, the total amount the family had saved was $687. By how much was the actual savings more than the planned savings?

- $57.00
- $81.00
- $157.50
- $207.00
- $214.50

Family Savings

A family had a goal to save $1,890 over the course of a year by making equal monthly deposits into a savings account. At the end of the fourth month, the total amount the family had saved was $687. By how much was the actual savings more than the planned savings?

- $57.00
- $81.00
- $157.50
- $207.00
- $214.50

Explanation

The family's goal of $1,890 was to be divided in 12 equal payments, so each equal monthly payment was, according to the goal, supposed to be

$$payment = \frac{1890}{12}$$

If they had stuck to this plan, the would have made this payment 4 times, so far, by the end of the fourth month, giving us

$$4(payment) = 4\left(\frac{1890}{12}\right)$$

$$= \frac{4}{12} 1890$$

$$= \frac{1}{3} 1890 = 630$$

They gave $687 instead, so they have exceeded their goal so far by $687 - 630 = 57$ dollars.

The correct answer is (A).

Two rectangular table tops have equal area. If the first table top is 6 feet by 18 feet and the second table top is 9 feet wide, what is the length of the second table top, in feet?

- $7\frac{1}{2}$
- 9
- $11\frac{3}{4}$
- 12
- 24

EQUAL RECTANGULAR AREAS

Two rectangular table tops have equal area. If the first table top is 6 feet by 18 feet and the second table top is 9 feet wide, what is the length of the second table top, in feet?

- $7\frac{1}{2}$
- 9
- $11\frac{3}{4}$
- 12
- 24

EXPLANATION

Since these areas are each length times width and are equal, the question is telling us that

$$6 \times 18 = ? \times 9$$

Dividing both sides by 9, we have an equation equivalent to:

$$6 \times 2 = ?$$

Therefore, the missing dimension is 12. The correct answer is (D).

Which of the following is the value of $(\sqrt{0.0081})^{\frac{1}{2}}$?

- 0.003
- 0.009
- 0.03
- 0.09
- 0.3

Radical and Power

Which of the following is the value of $(\sqrt{0.0081})^{\frac{1}{2}}$?

- 0.003
- 0.009
- 0.03
- 0.09
- 0.3

Explanation

A square root is equivalent to the $\frac{1}{2}$ power, so the expression we are given is equivalent to

$$\left((0.0081)^{\frac{1}{2}}\right)^{\frac{1}{2}}$$

It's often a good idea to convert a square root into an exponent of power 1/2, because then you can use exponent rules. Such as now: exponents of exponents multiply, so we have

$$(0.0081)^{\frac{1}{4}}$$

We can write the inside of the parentheses as

$$(81 \times 10^{-4})^{\frac{1}{4}}$$

If these rules are foreign to you, you may want to consult the GMAT Free *Math Review*. Since the two terms inside the parenthesis are multiplied, we can distribute the exponent:

$$(81)^{\frac{1}{4}}(10^{-4})^{\frac{1}{4}}$$

The left factor is now the fourth root of 81, which is the square root of the square root of 81, which is the square root of 9, which is 3. In the right factor, we once again multiply exponents:

$$3(10^{-1}) = \frac{3}{10} = 0.3$$

We have our answer: choice (E).

This question can be solved less formally, but just as exactly, by starting with the inside of the radical with the following reasoning. The square root of 81 is 9, and there are 4 decimal places inside the radical, so expression is equal to 0.09 to the power 1/2. Using that same reasoning again, we can see that the answer must be 0.3. The correct answer is (E).

During the last two minutes before a lecture began, the number of occupied seats in an auditorium increased from 112 to 135. If the number of occupied seats at the beginning of the lecture was 75 percent of total capacity, how many seats in the auditorium were empty two minutes prior to the lecture?

- 14
- 22
- 36
- 44
- 68

Lecture Hall Seats

During the last two minutes before a lecture began, the number of occupied seats in an auditorium increased from 112 to 135. If the number of occupied seats at the beginning of the lecture was 75 percent of total capacity, how many seats in the auditorium were empty two minutes prior to the lecture?

- 14
- 22
- 36
- 44
- 68

Explanation

In this question, the "number of occupied seats at the beginning of the lecture" was 135, since there was no further time for anyone else to come in or leave. And that number is 75 percent of the total capacity:

$$135 = 0.75C,$$

where we have named the capacity C. We know that the 0.75 goes on the right side of the equation because, in expressing the sentence as algebra, the word "is" in "135 is 75 percent of" will mean an equal sign.

To solve for C, we must isolate it. One way to do this is to convert 0.75 into a fraction and multiply both side of the equation by its reciprocal.

$$135 = 0.75C$$

$$135 = \frac{3}{4}C$$

$$\left(\frac{4}{3}\right)135 = \left(\frac{3}{4}C\right)\left(\frac{4}{3}\right)$$

$$\left(\frac{4}{3}\right)135 = \left(\frac{3}{4} \times \frac{4}{3}\right)C$$

$$\left(\frac{4}{3}\right)135 = C$$

$$\frac{540}{3} = C$$

$$180 = C.$$

We have found the seating capacity: it's 180. The question asks for how many were empty two minutes prior to the lecture. At that time, 112 seats were filled, so the number empty was $180 - 112 = 68$. The correct answer is (E).

Rectangular Floor X is to be half as long as it is wide. If its perimeter is to be 240 yards, what will be the length of Floor X, in yards?

- 20
- 40
- 60
- 80
- 120

Rectangular Floor

Rectangular Floor X is to be half as long as it is wide. If its perimeter is to be 240 yards, what will be the length of Floor X, in yards?

- 20
- 40
- 60
- 80
- 120

Explanation

Let's call the length and width of this floor L and W. The length is half, so we have $2L = W$. We can confirm that W is larger in that equation, so the 2 is on the correct side. The perimeter is 240, so we also have $2L + 2W = 240$. We can solve by substituting; since $2L = W$, then the equation for perimeter becomes $W + 2W = 240$. Therefore, $3W = 240$ and $W = 80$. We have found the width! The question is asking for the length, which is half the width, so it is 40.

The correct answer is (B).

Of an inventory of a particular item received at a store, one week, $\frac{1}{2}$ was sold the first day, $\frac{1}{3}$ on the second day, and $\frac{1}{8}$ the third day. If the store succeeds in selling the remaining 7 units, how many units in total will it have sold?

- 120
- 144
- 168
- 184
- 196

FRACTIONS OF INVENTORY

Of an inventory of a particular item received at a store, one week, $\frac{1}{2}$ was sold the first day, $\frac{1}{3}$ on the second day, and $\frac{1}{8}$ the third day. If the store succeeds in selling the remaining 7 units, how many units in total will it have sold?

- 120
- 144
- 168
- 184
- 196

EXPLANATION

This question describes three fraction of a particular amount of inventory. Notice that, on the second day, it's saying that a third of the *original* inventory was sold, not a third of the remaining inventory after the first day, since those two interpretations will lead to different results. So half the inventory plus a third of the inventory plus an eighth of the inventory adds up to a number that is seven less than the inventory. If the inventory is X, then that means

$$\frac{X}{2} + \frac{X}{3} + \frac{X}{8} = X - 7.$$

The fractions can be eliminated by multiplying both sides of the equation by 24. Or you can give the fractions on the left a common denominator of 24:

$$\frac{12X}{24} + \frac{8X}{24} + \frac{3X}{24} = X - 7$$

$$\frac{23X}{24} = X - 7$$

We are now getting somewhere with this equation, because $\frac{23}{24}$ is all of the inventory except 7 units. In other words 7 is $\frac{1}{24}$ of the inventory. The total inventory is, therefore, $24 \times 7 = 140 + 28 = 168$. The correct answer is (C).

This question can be solved efficiently in a number of different ways, some closely similar, some more different. For example, we basically cut off the algebra when we realized that 7 had to be $\frac{1}{24}$ of the total inventory. If we hadn't noticed that, we could have proceeded with solving $\frac{23X}{24} = X - 7$ in a more brute-force manner by multiplying both sides by 24, subtracting $23X$ from both sides and adding 24×7 to both sides, and finding that $24 \times 7 = X$. That finish is mathematically identical, although for most people it is easier to make an error along this path and also more difficult to figure out what the error was. Another method is to solve backwards. A great many GMAT questions can be solved purely backwards. You can start with 144, and see whether half of it plus a third of it plus an eighth of it yields $144 - 7$. This method is sometimes far and away the most efficient way to solve a GMAT question, while sometimes an algebraic method is only viable method, so you will want to cultivate both methods. The correct answer is (C).

When $\frac{1}{10}$ percent of 10,000 is added to $\frac{1}{10}$ of 10,000, the result is

- 0
- 200
- 1000
- 1010
- 2000

One-Tenth Percent

When $\frac{1}{10}$ percent of 10,000 is added to $\frac{1}{10}$ of 10,000, the result is

- 0
- 200
- 1000
- 1010
- 2000

Explanation

Our first step is to express these words purely in numbers. "$\frac{1}{10}$ percent of 10,000" is

$$\left(\frac{1}{10}\right)\left(\frac{1}{100}\right) 10{,}000.$$

We know we need that $\frac{1}{100}$ in there because we are talking about not $\frac{1}{10}$, but rather $\frac{1}{10}$ percent. This gives us

$$\frac{10{,}000}{1000} = 10.$$

There are four zeros on the top and three on the bottom, so they all cancel except for one zero on top.

The second part of our sum is "$\frac{1}{10}$ of 10,000," or

$$\left(\frac{1}{10}\right) 10{,}000 = \frac{10{,}000}{10} = 1{,}000.$$

When we add these two terms, we get 1,010. The correct answer is (D).

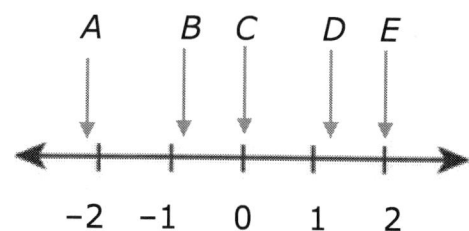

Which of the points indicated by the labels A, B, C, D, and E on the number line above has the second-least absolute value?

- A
- B
- C
- D
- E

Absolute Value on Number Line

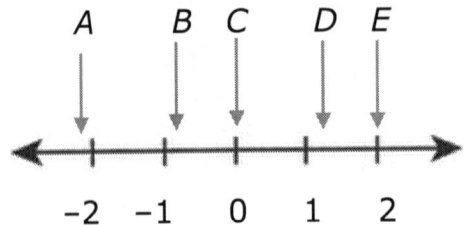

Which of the points indicated by the labels A, B, C, D, and E on the number line above has the second-least absolute value?

- A
- B
- C
- D
- E

Explanation

Absolute value is best thought of as distance from zero. The point here with the smallest distance from zero is C. The point with the second-least distance from zero is B. The distance from zero of C is zero, or close to zero. The distance from zero of B is a little less than 1, and the distance from zero of D is a little more than 1. The correct answer is (B).

One person bought 3 packages of fresh fish costing an average (arithmetic mean) of $12.40, and another person bought 6 packages of fresh fish costing an average of $15.25. What was the average cost, rounded to the nearest cent, of all of the packages of fresh fish?

- $12.75
- $13.33
- $13.50
- $13.83
- $14.30

GFPS13

Fresh Fish Average of Averages

One person bought 3 packages of fresh fish costing an average (arithmetic mean) of $12.40, and another person bought 6 packages of fresh fish costing an average of $15.25. What was the average cost, rounded to the nearest cent, of all of the packages of fresh fish?

- $12.75
- $13.33
- $13.50
- $13.83
- $14.30

Explanation

Since average of items $= \frac{\text{sum of items}}{\text{number of items}}$, it is equally true that

$$\text{sum of items} = (\text{average of items})(\text{number of items}).$$

We can apply this fact multiple times. First, we can write it twice for each of the given averages:

$$\text{sum of items \#1} = (12.40)(3) = 36 + 1.20 = 37.20$$

$$\text{sum of items \#2} = (15.25)(6) = 60 + 30 + 1.50 = 91.50$$

Then, we can write for the group of items overall:

$$\text{sum of items} = 37.20 + 91.50 = (\text{average of items})(9)$$

$$\text{average of items} = \frac{128.70}{9}$$

Then we can bust out our long-division skills to determine the right side of this equation.

```
        1   4.
    ┌─────────────
  9 │ 1   2   8.  7   0
        9
      ─────
        3   8
        3   6
      ─────
            2
```

We can actually pause here, since 14 point something leaves only one possible answer. The correct answer is (E). Another way to solve this question is to consider that the average of the two groups will be substantially above the midpoint between the numbers 12.40 and 15.25, but less than 15.25. This is because there are 3 numbers in each group evenly balancing each other out on either side of that midpoint, with then three items remaining in the higher group pulling the average upward.

The people who entered a room received upon entering distinct, consecutive identification numbers from 1000 to 1249. What is the probability that a person in the room selected at random will have an identification number with a hundreds digit of 1?

- $\dfrac{2}{5}$
- $\dfrac{2}{7}$
- $\dfrac{33}{83}$
- $\dfrac{99}{250}$
- $\dfrac{100}{249}$

IDENTIFICATION NUMBERS

The people who entered a room received upon entering distinct, consecutive identification numbers from 1000 to 1249. What is the probability that a person in the room selected at random will have an identification number with a hundreds digit of 1?

- $\frac{2}{5}$
- $\frac{2}{7}$
- $\frac{33}{83}$
- $\frac{99}{250}$
- $\frac{100}{249}$

EXPLANATION

In this question, the room and the entering of the room is not so important. Rather the point is that there are people numbered 1000 to 1249. If we choose one person at random, the probability that that person will have a number with a hundreds digit of 1 will be

$$\frac{\text{number of ID's with a hundreds digit of 1}}{\text{total number of ID's}}$$

The total number of ID's is 1249 − 1000 + 1 = 250. We can be sure of this by experimenting with smaller numbers. For example, if the ID's went from 1000 to 1001, the difference would be 1, but there would be 2 ID's, and so forth. Based on this alone, we can conclude right off the bat that the correct answer must be (A) or (D), since a denominator of 250 couldn't reduce to any of the other denominators (since they are not factors of 250).

As for the numerator: the number of ID's with a hundreds digit of 1 is the group from 1100 up to 1199. That is 1199 − 1100 + 1 = 100 ID's. Therefore:

$$\frac{\text{number of ID's with a hundreds digit of 1}}{\text{total number of ID's}} = \frac{100}{250}$$

Both the numerator and denominator can be divided by 50 to the simplest form of the fraction, $\frac{2}{5}$. The correct answer is (A).

Upon making a sale, Pat receives a 9 percent commission on the price of the item in excess of $9,000. If Pat's commission on a sale was $405, what was the price of the item?

- $9,600
- $11,100
- $13,500
- $14,400
- $16,500

Commission on Sales

Upon making a sale, Pat receives a 9 percent commission on the price of the item in excess of $9,000. If Pat's commission on a sale was $405, what was the price of the item?

- $9,600
- $11,100
- $13,500
- $14,400
- $16,500

Explanation

If we call the price of the item sold P, then the excess of $9,000 of the price is $P - 9,000$. Whenever writing an algebraic expression such as this, if you can think of a concrete example on hand to try, that's an easy way to confirm that your algebra is correct. For example, if the price were 10,000, then $P = 10,000$ and $P - 9,000 = 10,000 - 9,000 = 1,000$ and it all makes sense, so the expression is correct. We're told 9% of this amount is Pat's commission, so we have the equation

$$0.09(P - 9,000) = 405$$

We must solve for P. It's worth checking the answer choices; maybe plugging one in would be much easier than solving for the answer, but probably not in this case.

$$\frac{9}{100}(P - 9,000) = 405$$

We can convert decimals into fractions, because math with fractions has ample opportunities to simplify.

$$\frac{100}{9} \cdot \frac{9}{100}(P - 9,000) = (405)\frac{100}{9}$$

$$(P - 9,000) = (405)\frac{100}{9}$$

There is a divisibility by 9 trick: if the digits of a number add to 9, the number is divisible by 9, so 405 ($4 + 0 + 5 = 9$) is divisible by 9.

$$(P - 9,000) = (9 \times 45)\frac{100}{9}$$

$$P - 9,000 = 4500$$

$$P = 13,500$$

We have our answer. We can double-check that it makes sense: the amount in excess of $9,000 is $4,500, and her commission was a bit less than 10%, so a bit less than $450, so $405 makes sense. The correct answer is (C).

A rectangular box has a volume of 320 cubic meters, and a second box is half as long, half as wide, and one quarter as high as the first one. What is the volume, in cubic meters, of the second box?

- 20
- 40
- 64
- 80
- 160

Volume of Two Boxes

A rectangular box has a volume of 320 cubic meters, and a second box is half as long, half as wide, and one quarter as high as the first one. What is the volume, in cubic meters, of the second box?

- 20
- 40
- 64
- 80
- 160

Explanation

The first box has a volume of 320 cubic meters, and this could be obtained through various different possible cases of exact dimensions. For example, the box could be $16 \times 2 \times 10$ or $8 \times 4 \times 10$. But there is something interesting about this question: the correct answer, evidently, doesn't depend on the exact dimension of the first box, because we don't know what they are, and there is a single, definitive, correct answer to this question. This type of situation crops up frequently on GMAT questions: we are dealing with a range of possible cases and an outcome that is the same for all the cases. When this is the case, we are free to choose any particular case we want, for our own convenience. For example, since we are going to be taking a half, a half, and a quarter, we can imagine a box that has a volume

$$320 = 8 \times 10 \times 4$$

Then, the volume of the second box is

$$\left(\frac{1}{2}\right) 8 \times \left(\frac{1}{2}\right) 10 \times \left(\frac{1}{2}\right) 4$$

$$4 \times 5 \times 1 = 20$$

Therefore, the correct answer is (A).

This technique might seem too good to be true. Or it might strike you as clear enough, but you doubt that you'll be able to replicate it. The key is, before automatically jumping into algebra, to consider the range of possible cases. Analysis by cases is critical in data sufficiency, and it's useful anywhere logical thinking is required. It's a useful step in most questions to consider briefly what the range of possible cases is for the question. Sometimes, you'll find that you can choose any one of those possible cases, or you can choose two cases and compare them. The correct answer is (A).

What is the 30th digit to the right of the decimal point in the decimal form of $\frac{3}{11}$?

- ○ 2
- ○ 3
- ○ 5
- ○ 6
- ○ 7

30TH DIGIT

What is the 30th digit to the right of the decimal point in the decimal form of $\frac{3}{11}$?

- 2
- 3
- 5
- 6
- 7

EXPLANATION

If this question, or any GMAT question, strikes you as impossible when you first encounter it, do not despair. The GMAT is not all about tricks – they are probably better described as puzzles – but they are like magic tricks in a way: if you don't know the trick, it can seem magical and mysterious, but when you understand the trick, it's simple. Through practice, the appearance of magic will disappear and you will be the one waving the wand.

Whenever we have a fraction that we need to convert into a decimal, if the conversion is not obvious or we don't know a shortcut, we can always try long division. A fraction represents division, so $\frac{3}{11}$ represents 3 divided by 11, and we can actually perform this division by hand through long division.

$$\begin{array}{r} 0.272 \\ 11 \overline{\smash{)}3.000} \\ \underline{22} \\ 80 \\ \underline{77} \\ 30 \end{array}$$

We can actually pause here, because there is a pattern that will repeat. The digits 2 and 7 will alternate, so $\frac{3}{11} = 0.\overline{27}$. This result makes sense, since $\frac{3}{11}$ has a slightly larger denominator than $\frac{3}{10}$, so it should be slightly smaller than 0.3.

We can determine the 30th number to the right of the decimal point from the pattern. The first digit to the right is a 2, the second digit to the right is a 7, and the third digit is a 2. Evidently, the odd places have a 2 and the even places have a 7. The 30th place is an even place, so the digit there will be a 7.

The correct answer is (E).

If $\left|x - \frac{3}{4}\right| < \frac{9}{4}$, which of the following could be a value of x?

- −3
- −2
- 2
- 3
- 6

Absolute Value Inequality

If $\left|x - \frac{3}{4}\right| < \frac{9}{4}$, which of the following could be a value of x?

- ○ −3
- ○ −2
- ○ 2
- ○ 3
- ○ 6

Explanation

This question concerns absolute value, which is best thought of as the distance of something from zero. In this question, the distance of $x - \frac{3}{4}$ from zero is less than $\frac{9}{4}$. In this question, and in every question with absolute value, there are two possible cases: the distance in question can be either to the left or to the right. For example, if $x - \frac{3}{4}$ is on the left side of 0, then it's a negative quantity. And if the distance is less than $\frac{9}{4}$ than, in this case, the left-side case,

$$x - \frac{3}{4} > -\frac{9}{4},$$

because it must be right of $-\frac{9}{4}$ on the number line and that's what "greater than" means. We can further clarify this case by adding $\frac{3}{4}$ to both sides of the inequality, getting

$$x > -\frac{6}{4}$$

$$x > -\frac{3}{2}$$

Meanwhile, answer choices (A) and (B) are negative, but they are both *less* than $-\frac{3}{2}$, since they are to the left of −1.5 on the number line.

There is another case: the distance from zero could be on the right side, in positive numbers. Then,

$$x - \frac{3}{4} < \frac{9}{4}$$

$$x < \frac{12}{4}$$

$$x < 3$$

There is one answer choice that fits this case: (C). Note that, to evaluate absolute value, we break it into two cases, one positive and one negative, and in those cases the absolute value vertical bar notation is not required. The correct answer is (C).

Running at the same constant rate, 6 identical machines can produce a total of 33 widgets per hour. At this rate, how many widgets could 14 such machines produce in 3 hours?

- 66
- 231
- 462
- 693
- 909

MACHINES AND COMBINED RATE

Running at the same constant rate, 6 identical machines can produce a total of 33 widgets per hour. At this rate, how many widgets could 14 such machines produce in 3 hours?

- o 66
- o 231
- o 462
- o 693
- o 909

EXPLANATION

Rates are best expressed in fractions with units. The rate of the 6 equal machines is

$$6R = \frac{33 \text{ widgets}}{1 \text{ hour}},$$

where R is the rate of one machine working, since all machines work at an equal rate. To find the rate for 14 machines, not 6, we can multiply both sides of the equation by $\frac{14}{6}$:

$$\left(\frac{14}{6}\right)6R = \frac{33 \text{ widgets}}{1 \text{ hour}}\left(\frac{14}{6}\right)$$

$$14R = \frac{33 \text{ widgets}}{1 \text{ hour}}\left(\frac{14}{6}\right)$$

We now have 14 machines on the left as we want. The right side is going to give us 6 hours on the right if we multiply it out, but we want 3 hours, so we can multiply the right side by 1 ...

$$14R = \frac{33 \text{ widgets}}{1 \text{ hour}}\left(\frac{14}{6}\right)\left(\frac{\frac{1}{2}}{\frac{1}{2}}\right)$$

$$14R = \frac{33 \times 7 \text{ widgets}}{3 \text{ hours}}$$

$$14R = \frac{210 + 21 \text{ widgets}}{3 \text{ hours}} = \frac{231 \text{ widgets}}{3 \text{ hours}}$$

For 14 machines, we have 231 widgets in 3 hours.

We can make an estimate to check that this is in the ballpark. The original 6 machines made 33 widgets in 1 hour. And 14 is more than double the number of machines, so they are doing something over 66 widgets an hour. And they are working for 3 hours, so the result will be something like 66 or 70 times 3, so around 210 widgets per hour. Indeed, we could have used that method to start and gotten the answer very quickly, because there is only one answer choice even close to the estimate.

The correct answer is (B).

A foot race had 36 teams of a dozen runners each. By noon, $\frac{4}{9}$ of the teams had finished the race, and 70 percent of the remaining teams finished the race by one o' clock. How many teams had not finished the race by one o' clock?

- 1
- 2
- 4
- 6
- 8

Teams Finishing Foot Race

A foot race had 36 teams of a dozen runners each. By noon, $\frac{4}{9}$ of the teams had finished the race, and 70 percent of the remaining teams finished the race by one o' clock. How many teams had not finished the race by one o' clock?

- 1
- 2
- 4
- 6
- 8

Explanation

In this question, the number of runners on each team has been given to us, but it doesn't seem to be important. We are asked how many teams finished, and all of useful information given to us is in terms of teams.

Since we have 36 teams, and $\frac{4}{9}$ of them finished by noon, the number that finished by noon is

$$(36)\frac{4}{9} = (9 \times 4)\frac{4}{9} = 16$$

Then, we are told, 70% of the *remaining* teams finished. How many were remaining after 16 finished? The number remaining was 20, since 36 − 16 = 20. So 70% of 20 teams finished by one o'clock. That number is

$$0.7(20) = 14$$

Note that, in both statements, the fraction "of" a number or the percent "of" a number indicates multiplication of the fraction or percent by that number. Anyway, 14 of the remaining 20 just finished, so there are 6 teams that haven't finished yet. That's what the question is asking for.

The correct answer is (D).

$(0.1)^0 + (0.1)^1 + (0.1)^2 + (0.1)^3 =$

- 0.1
- 1.111
- 1.1211
- 1.2341
- 3.3

Powers of Tenth

$(0.1)^0 + (0.1)^1 + (0.1)^2 + (0.1)^3 =$

- 0.1
- 1.111
- 1.1211
- 1.2341
- 3.3

Explanation

A rule of thumb when we are dealing with any exponents is to convert everything possible into an exponent form, so that we can use exponent rules. Here we have a bunch of 0.1's, and they all can be written as 10^{-1}:

$$(10^{-1})^0 + (10^{-1})^1 + (10^{-1})^2 + (10^{-1})^3$$

Exponents of exponents multiply. (If you're rusty on this, see the GMAT Free *Math Review*.) So we have:

$$10^0 + 10^{-1} + 10^{-2} + 10^{-3}$$

Now we can get this expression out of exponent mode. Exponents of 10 basically count zeros or decimal places. The first term is 1 (and anything to the zeroth power is 1), and we have

$$1 + 0.1 + 0.01 + 0.001 = 1.111$$

Therefore, the correct answer is (B).

Note: just glancing at this question, you could have seen that the first term is one, because of the zero power, and that the other terms were small, so that the answer probably had to lie between (B) and (D), though it's not too much extra work to determine the correct answer definitively.

Again, the correct answer is (B).

180 is what percent of 20?

- 11%
- 30%
- 90%
- 600%
- 900%

PERCENT OF A NUMBER

180 is what percent of 20?

- 11%
- 30%
- 90%
- 600%
- 900%

EXPLANATION

The word "is" here is like an equal sign in a word, so we can express this question in algebra as

$$180 = (what\ percent)20$$

More precisely, "what percent" must be expressed as a decimal, or as a number over 100. Since the answer choices are expressed as percents (with a percent sign), the latter route is better for this question, so the accurate expression is

$$180 = \left(\frac{percent}{100}\right)20$$

$$9 = \left(\frac{percent}{100}\right)$$

$$percent = 900$$

This sounds like an awfully high percent, but it's correct: 180 is nine times as big as 20, so it's 900% of 20. The correct answer is (E).

Of the 50 members of a staff, 40 percent worked the day shift and the remaining 60 percent worked the night shift in a given week. Of the staff members, 80 percent prefer working the day shift and the remaining 20 percent prefer working the night shift. What is the minimum number of staff members who failed to receive his or her preference of shift that week?

- 15
- 17
- 20
- 25
- 30

Day Shift and Night Shift

Of the 50 members of a staff, 40 percent worked the day shift and the remaining 60 percent worked the night shift in a given week. Of the staff members, 80 percent prefer working the day shift and the remaining 20 percent prefer working the night shift. What is the minimum number of staff members who failed to receive his or her preference of shift that week?

- 15
- 17
- 20
- 25
- 30

Explanation

We're talking about two shifts here. In the given week, we have:

Staff	50
Day shift	0.4(50) = 20
Night shift	30

We want to know the minimum number of people who *didn't* get their preferences this week. We can calculate how many people prefer each shift:

Staff	50
Prefer day shift	0.8(50) = 40
Prefer night shift	10

The minimum of people not getting their preferences will also be the situation in which the maximum *do* get their preference. So, say all 20 people who worked day shift preferred it. That leaves 40 − 20 = 20 people who prefer the night shift who didn't get it. And there are 10 people left in the group of 50, but they worked the night shift and 10 people prefer the night shift, so those 10 got their preference. Therefore, 20 people didn't get their preference.

The correct answer is (C).

The rates of import tax on six of the last seven items Leo imported were 13%, 16%, 11%, 17%, 12%, and 14%, respectively. If the tax rate on the seventh item was either 17%, 15%, or 14%, for which of the three values does the average (arithmetic mean) tax rate per item for the seven items equal the median tax rate for the seven items?

I. 17%

II. 15%

III. 14%

- II only
- III only
- I and II only
- II and III only
- I, II, and III

Import Taxes

The rates of import tax on six of the last seven items Leo imported were 13%, 16%, 11%, 17%, 12%, and 14%, respectively. If the tax rate on the seventh item was either 17%, 15%, or 14%, for which of the three values does the average (arithmetic mean) tax rate per item for the seven items equal the median tax rate for the seven items?

I. 17%

II. 15%

III. 14%

- o II only
- o III only
- o I and II only
- o II and III only
- o I, II, and III

Explanation

The six rates listed are a set of numbers, which we can order and write without the percentage signs:

$$\{11, 12, 13, 14, 16, 17\}$$

Each of the Roman numerals listed in the question is a different case – a different value of the seventh number that goes in the set. Case I: the number that we add into the set is 17. So then, the ordered set is:

$$\{11, 12, 13, 14, 16, 17, 17\}$$

We are asked whether the average, or mean, equals the median. The median is easier to find, so we can start there. The middle number is 14, so that's the median. That will be the average if all the differences of the numbers from 14 cancel out. For example, the 11 and the last 17 cancel out, because they are a −3 and a +3. But the others don't cancel out. They are −2, −1, and +2, +3 so they net to +2, not zero. Therefore Case I is out. The median and mean are different, so Roman numeral I is not in the correct answer.

Case II: the final number is a 15, giving us this set:

$$\{11, 12, 13, 14, 15, 16, 17\}$$

We can see pretty quickly here that the median equals the mean, because 14 is the median, and the other numbers balance out around 14 in pairs – 11 with 17, 12, with 16, and so on. So II is in the correct answer. We have narrowed to answer choices (A) and (C), but we still must look at Case III.

Case III: the last number is 14. That gives us the set

$$\{11, 12, 13, 14, 14, 16, 17\}$$

Again, 14 is the median. So again, the 11 and the 17 cancel each other, as do the 12 and the 16. But the differences from the would-be mean of 14 don't cancel for 13 and 14, so the mean isn't 14. Therefore III is out, and the answer is II only. The correct answer is (A).

If n is a prime number greater than 3, what is the remainder when n^2 is divided by 6?

- 0
- 1
- 2
- 3
- 5

Prime Number and Remainder

If n is a prime number greater than 3, what is the remainder when n^2 is divided by 6?

- 0
- 1
- 2
- 3
- 5

Explanation

We can approach this question through analysis of possible cases. The variable n could be 5. In that case, $n^2 = 25$ and $\frac{25}{6} = 4\frac{1}{6}$, so the remainder is 1. In another possible case, n could be 7. In that case, $n^2 = 49$ and $\frac{49}{6} = 8\frac{1}{6}$. The remainder is again 1. From the way the question is written, it must be true that 1 is the remainder for all prime numbers greater than 3, since we know there is one and only one correct answer to any GMAT question.

The correct answer is (B).

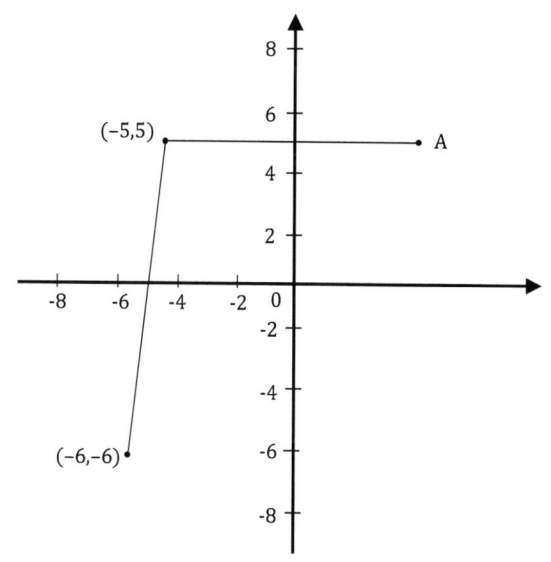

In the figure above, the coordinates of point A are

- (5,−5)
- (−5,5)
- (6,6)
- (6,−5)
- (6,5)

Points in Coordinate Plane

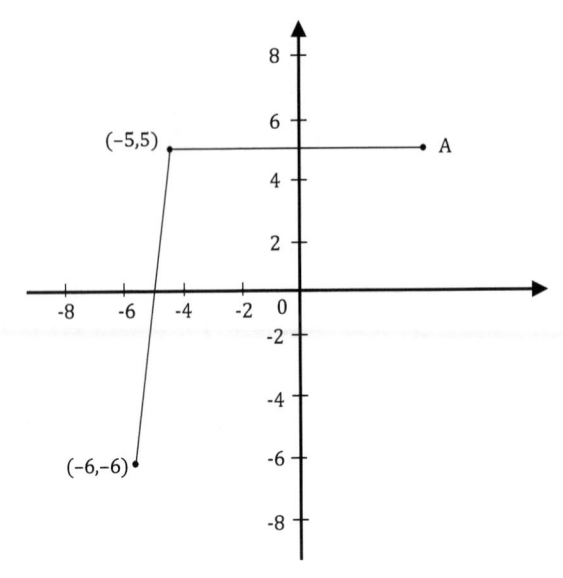

In the figure above, the coordinates of point A are

- (5,−5)
- (−5,5)
- (6,6)
- (6,−5)
- (6,5)

Explanation

We can see that the line at the top of this graph is parallel to the *y*-axis, because it includes the point (−5,5) and also crosses the *x*-axis at a height of 5. Therefore, point A must have a *y*-value of 5. There is only one answer choice with that *y* value and a positive *x*-value, (E).

The correct answer is (E).

The ratio 3 to $\frac{1}{4}$ is equal to the ratio

- 12 to 1
- 7 to 1
- 4 to 3
- 3 to 4
- 1 to 12

Ratio with a Fraction

The ratio 3 to $\frac{1}{4}$ is equal to the ratio

- 12 to 1
- 7 to 1
- 4 to 3
- 3 to 4
- 1 to 12

Explanation

Ratios with two parts are usually best expressed as fractions. The word "to" can be thought of as delineating the bar of the fraction. So the ratio of 3 to $\frac{1}{4}$ is

$$\frac{3}{\frac{1}{4}}$$

To simplify any fraction, we can multiply the top and the bottom by the same thing, so anything over anything equals 1 and therefore the action is equivalent to multiplying by 1:

$$\frac{3}{\frac{1}{4}} \times \frac{4}{4} = \frac{12}{1}$$

Converting from fraction terminology back to English, this final fraction is "12 to 1." By comparing the number order of the original phrase, we see that 12 corresponds to 3 (both are numerators) and therefore 12 to 1 is correct, not 1 to 12.

The correct answer is (A).

A student's average (arithmetic mean) test score on 4 tests is 68. What must be the student's score on a 5th test for the student's average score on the 5 tests to be 70?

- 70
- 72
- 74
- 76
- 78

Average with Additional Item

A student's average (arithmetic mean) test score on 4 tests is 68. What must be the student's score on a 5th test for the student's average score on the 5 tests to be 70?

- 70
- 72
- 74
- 76
- 78

Explanation

This question is about averages. Typically, average questions are made easier by working with the sums, using the twist on the average equation:

$$\text{sum of items} = (\text{average of items})(\text{number of items}).$$

From the first 4 tests, we have

$$\text{sum of items} = (68)(4) = 240 + 32 = 272.$$

Using this equation again separately, if the fifth test gives an overall average of 70, then

$$\text{sum of 5 items} = (70)(5) = 350.$$

The difference of the sums is $350 - 272 = 78$, so that would have to be the fifth test score to meet the condition stated by the question. The correct answer is (E).

$$\frac{1}{1-\frac{1}{3}} - \frac{1}{1-\frac{1}{2}} =$$

- $-\frac{1}{3}$
- $-\frac{1}{2}$
- $-\frac{1}{12}$
- $\frac{1}{12}$
- $\frac{1}{3}$

Subtracting Compound Fractions

$$\frac{1}{1-\frac{1}{3}} - \frac{1}{1-\frac{1}{2}} =$$

- $-\frac{1}{3}$
- $-\frac{1}{2}$
- $-\frac{1}{12}$
- $\frac{1}{12}$
- $\frac{1}{3}$

Explanation

We have an expression here with two fractions in it. We can evaluate the denominators directly to get:

$$\frac{1}{\frac{2}{3}} - \frac{1}{\frac{1}{2}} = ?$$

The number 1 over a fraction equals that fraction flipped. You can prove this to yourself by multiplying the first fraction by $\frac{3}{2}$ over $\frac{3}{2}$, for example. So we have

$$\frac{3}{2} - 2 = ?$$

The number 2 is $\frac{4}{2}$, so the left side is $-\frac{1}{2}$.

The correct answer is (B).

Coins worth $60.00 are divided into two piles. If one pile is worth $12.00 more than the other, what is the worth of the smaller pile?

- $5.00
- $12.00
- $24.00
- $36.00
- $72.00

PILES OF COINS

Coins worth $60.00 are divided into two piles. If one pile is worth $12.00 more than the other, what is the worth of the smaller pile?

- $5.00
- $12.00
- $24.00
- $36.00
- $72.00

EXPLANATION

We have coins and piles, but this question is more about piles. The answer choices look friendly, so let's work with those. Say we take (B). If the smaller pile is $12, then the larger pile is $12 + $12 = $24 but that would yield a total of $36, not $60. That smaller pile is too small. Looking at (D), $36 doesn't make sense as a smaller pile, because it's already more than half of $60. Therefore, the correct answer for the smaller pile must be the one between these possibilities, $24. We can check: $24 + 36 = $60.

The correct answer is (C).

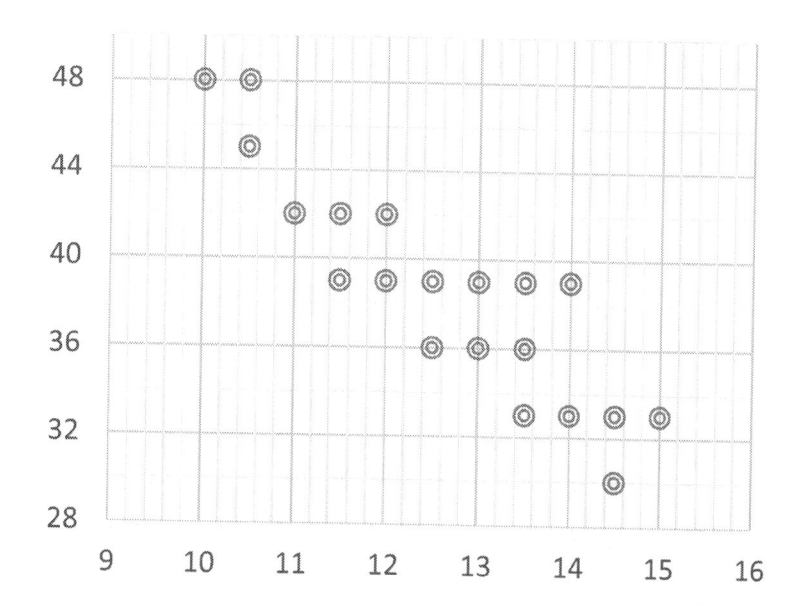

The dots on the graph above indicate number of months worked and the number of clients for the members of a service team. How many team members have worked at least one year and have more than 36 clients?

- 3
- 5
- 6
- 9
- 14

Graph of Hours Worked

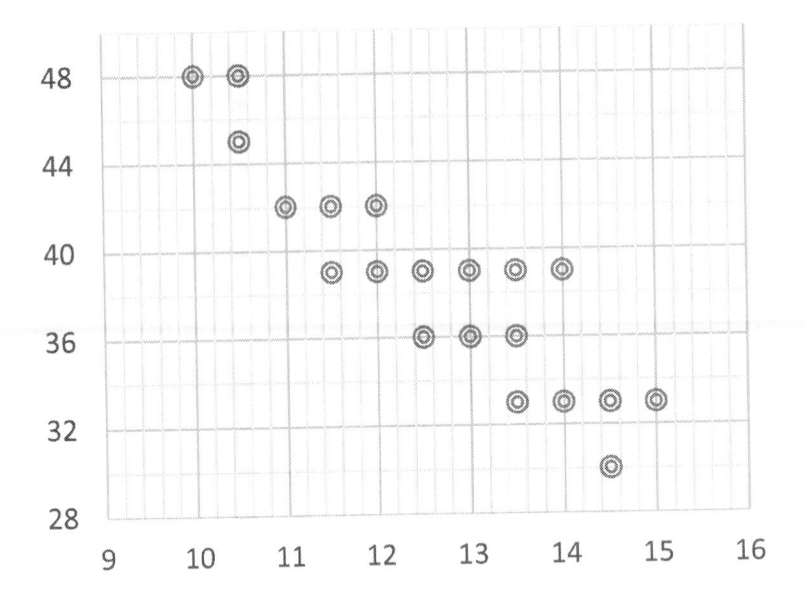

The dots on the graph above indicate number of months worked and the number of clients for the members of a service team. How many team members have worked at least one year and have more than 36 clients?

- 3
- 5
- 6
- 9
- 14

Explanation

The members who have worked 12 months or more and have over 36 clients are inside this box:

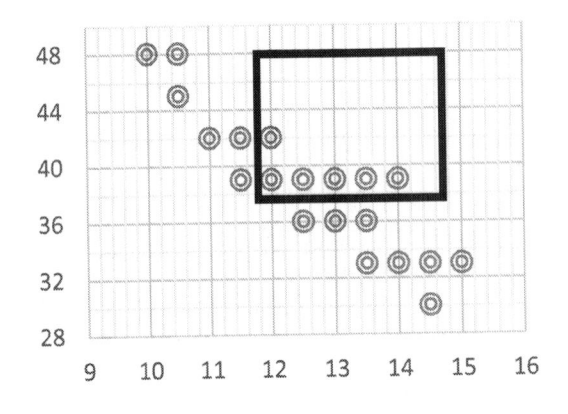

We count them up and find that they are 6. The correct answer is (C).

The value of an investment increased by 10 percent during the first year, increased by 5 percent during the second year, and decreased by 10 percent during the third year. What percent of the original value is the current value of the investment?

- 103.50%
- 103.95%
- 105.00%
- 115.00%
- 127.05%

Percent Increases and Decreases

The value of an investment increased by 10 percent during the first year, increased by 5 percent during the second year, and decreased by 10 percent during the third year. What percent of the original value is the current value of the investment?

- 103.50%
- 103.95%
- 105.00%
- 115.00%
- 127.05%

Explanation

In this question, the correct answer does not depend on the value of the investment, so we can work with the case in which the investment is $100. In the first year, it increases by 10% to $110. Then it increases by 5%, and 5% of half of 10%, and we can move the decimal point to see that 10% of 110 is 11. So it increases by 5.5 from $110 to $115.5. In the final year, it decreases by 10%. Moving the decimal point, we can see that 10% of $115.5 is $11.55. Therefore, we have

$$\begin{array}{cccccc} & 1 & 1 & 5. & 5 & 0 \\ & & 1 & 1. & 5 & 5 \\ \hline & 1 & 0 & 3. & 9 & 5 \end{array}$$

The current value is $103.95, and the original value was $100. So the current value is 103.95% of the original value.

The correct answer is (B).

$\sqrt{(9)(15) + (5)(18)} =$

- $3\sqrt{20}$
- 15
- 25
- $3\sqrt{20} + 3\sqrt{10}$
- 34

Simplifying Radicals

$$\sqrt{(9)(15) + (5)(18)} =$$

- $3\sqrt{20}$
- 15
- 25
- $3\sqrt{20} + 3\sqrt{10}$
- 34

Explanation

The two terms added under this square root cannot be separated into square roots. That's a common error in dealing with radicals. However, terms that are multiplied by each other can be separated into square roots. And we can get two terms that are multiplied by each other by pulling out a common factor.

$$\sqrt{9 \times (15 + (5)(2))}$$

$$\sqrt{9} \times \sqrt{(15) + (5)(2)}$$

Now we have two terms that are easy to simplify further:

$$3 \times \sqrt{25}$$

So we get $3 \times 5 = 15$. The correct answer is (B).

If it takes 65 minutes to drive s miles, how many minutes will it take to drive r miles at the same rate?

- $\dfrac{65r}{s}$
- $\dfrac{65s}{r}$
- $\dfrac{r}{65s}$
- $\dfrac{65}{rs}$
- $\dfrac{rs}{65}$

Driving at a Constant Rate

If it takes 65 minutes to drive s miles, how many minutes will it take to drive r miles at the same rate?

- $\dfrac{65r}{s}$
- $\dfrac{65s}{r}$
- $\dfrac{r}{65s}$
- $\dfrac{65}{rs}$
- $\dfrac{rs}{65}$

Explanation

Here we have a rate question, so we can set it up with a fraction that includes the relevant units:

$$\frac{65 \text{ minutes}}{s \text{ miles}}$$

We want to get r miles in the denominator without changing the value of the rate, so we can multiply by a form of 1:

$$\frac{65 \text{ minutes}}{s \text{ miles}} \times \frac{\frac{r}{s}}{\frac{r}{s}}$$

The s's in the denominator cancel, leaving us with r miles. The numerator becomes $\frac{65r}{s}$ minutes. Therefore,

The correct answer is (A).

How many hours does it take Jay to paint *p* rooms if he paints at the rate of *q* rooms per hour?

- $\dfrac{p}{q}$
- $\dfrac{q}{p}$
- pq
- $\dfrac{60p}{q}$
- $\dfrac{q}{60p}$

Jay's Painting Rate

How many hours does it take Jay to paint p rooms if he paints at the rate of q rooms per hour?

- $\frac{p}{q}$
- $\frac{q}{p}$
- pq
- $\frac{60p}{q}$
- $\frac{q}{60p}$

Explanation

We can express Jay's painting rate as a fraction. It's always useful to write the units in the fraction.

$$\frac{q \text{ rooms}}{1 \text{ hour}}$$

We want to know how long it takes to paint p rooms, so we want a fraction like this with p in the numerator, not q. But we don't want to change the value of fraction, because Jay's rate is not changing in this situation. So we can multiply the fraction by 1 in the form of $\frac{p}{q}$ over $\frac{p}{q}$:

$$\frac{q \text{ rooms}}{1 \text{ hour}} \times \frac{\frac{p}{q}}{\frac{p}{q}} = \frac{p \text{ rooms}}{\frac{p}{q} \text{ hour}}$$

The q's cancel on top and we end up with p rooms, just as we wanted. The time it takes to paint p rooms is evidently $\frac{p}{q}$ hours. We can check that it makes sense by considering a case. If he paints at a rate of $q=3$ rooms per hour, and he's painting $p=9$ rooms, then it will take $\frac{9}{3} = 3$ hours to paint nine rooms. It checks out.

The correct answer is (A).

Which of the following equations is NOT equivalent to $8y^2 = (x+3)(x-3)$?

- $24y^2 = 3x^2 - 27$
- $16y^2 = (2x+6)(x-3)$
- $8y^2 + 9 = x^2$
- $4y^2 = x^2 - \frac{9}{2}$
- $y^2 = \frac{x^2-9}{8}$

ALGEBRAIC EQUIVALENCE

Which of the following equations is NOT equivalent to $8y^2 = (x+3)(x-3)$?

- $24y^2 = 3x^2 - 27$
- $16y^2 = (2x+6)(x-3)$
- $8y^2 + 9 = x^2$
- $4y^2 = x^2 - \frac{9}{2}$
- $y^2 = \frac{x^2 - 9}{8}$

EXPLANATION

This question could obviously involve a lot of algebra, but we can analyze it by cases. Namely, we can examine a case of allowed variables of x and y. To make things as simple as possible, maybe we can have $y=2$, so that $8y^2 = 32$. That doesn't yield great values for x. Trying it the other way, if $(x+3)(x-3)$ were 8 and 2, so that $x = 5$, then $8y^2 = 16$ and $y^2 = 2$. Looking at the answer choices, working with y^2 directly should be manageable. So we have an allowed case: $y^2 = 2; x = 5$. Let's see how the answer choices hold up in this case:

$24(2) = 3(25) - 27$. That's $48 = 75 - 27$, which is true. So (A) is maybe equivalent to our starting equation.

$16(2) = (10 + 6)(2)$. That gives $32 = 32$, so (B) also may be equivalent to our starting equation.

$8(2) + 9 = 25$. That gives $16 + 9 = 25$, so (C) also may be equivalent to our starting equation.

$4(2) = 25 - \frac{9}{2}$. This is not true. So this equation is NOT equivalent to our starting equation. We can check (E) to be sure.

$2 = \frac{25-9}{8}$. That's true, so this equation may be equivalent to our starting equation.

We looked at a case that was allowed by our original equation, and it was allowed by all of the answer choices except (D). Therefore (D) must be the equation that is not equivalent to the original.

The correct answer is (D).

If the quotient $\frac{a}{b}$ is less than zero, which of the following CANNOT be true?

- $a > 0$
- $b > 0$
- $ab > 0$
- $a - b > 0$
- $a + b > 0$

Quotients of Positive and Negative Numbers

If the quotient $\frac{a}{b}$ is less than zero, which of the following CANNOT be true?

- $a > 0$
- $b > 0$
- $ab > 0$
- $a - b > 0$
- $a + b > 0$

Explanation

We are told that $\frac{a}{b}$ is negative. We don't know whether a in particular is positive or negative, but we can analyze the situation by cases. If a is positive, then b must be negative, in order for $\frac{a}{b}$ to be negative. If a is negative, then b must be positive, in order for $\frac{a}{b}$ to be negative. Similar cases hold when we start with b and consider a: one must be positive and one negative. This means that (C) cannot be true, because ab would only be positive if both numbers were positive or both numbers were negative.

The correct answer is (C).

$$\frac{1}{\frac{5}{4} - 2.5} =$$

- −0.8
- −1.25
- 1
- 1.25
- 0.8

Fractions, Decimals and Denominators

$$\frac{1}{\frac{5}{4} - 2.5} =$$

- −0.8
- −1.25
- 1
- 1.25
- 0.8

Explanation

To make sense of the denominator, we need either both fractions or both decimals. Fractions will be faster. The number 2.5 is $2\frac{1}{2}$, which is $\frac{5}{2}$, which is $\frac{10}{4}$. Therefore, we have

$$\frac{1}{\frac{5}{4} - \frac{10}{4}}$$

$$= \frac{1}{-\frac{5}{4}}$$

$$= -\frac{4}{5}$$

This last step is why it was easier to convert to fractions: because we can flip it (aka. multiply both the top and bottom by the inverse of the fraction) to get a proper fraction.

Our final fraction is equal to −0.8, so the correct answer is (A).

If $\frac{27}{0.5+y} = 6$, then $y =$

- −3.5
- 4
- 3
- 3.5
- 6

Variable in a Denominator

If $\frac{27}{0.5+y} = 6$, then $y =$

- −3.5
- 4
- 3
- 3.5
- 6

Explanation

The number 27 divided by something gives 6. So that something must be a little more than 4, since $6 \times 4 = 24$. That means that $y + 0.5$ is a bit more than 4. Given the answer choices, (B) is almost certainly the answer. Indeed, $6(4.5) = 24 + 3 = 27$.

The correct answer is (B).

At a wedding reception, each of 11 guests brought a different individual as a date. If 5 people leave the reception early, what is the greatest possible number of guests remaining with their original dates?

- 9
- 8
- 6
- 4
- 2

DATES AT A WEDDING RECEPTION

At a wedding reception, each of 11 guests brought a different individual as a date. If 5 people leave the reception early, what is the greatest possible number of guests remaining with their original dates?

- 9
- 8
- 6
- 4
- 2

EXPLANATION

In this socially awkward situation, guests are possibly leaving without their dates, and *vice versa*. We have 22 people total, and 5 people leave, so we have 17 people remaining. Since the date-guest groups are pairs, 8 guests maximum still have their date, with a stray person left who may be a guest or a date. That's the rosiest possible situation, as the question is asking for.

The correct answer is (B).

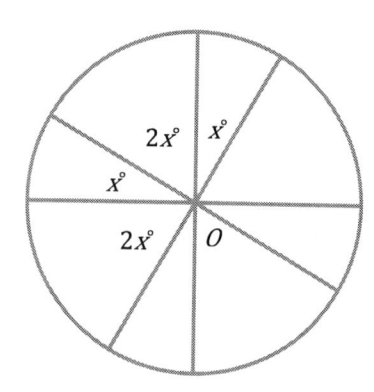

If O is the center of the circle above, what fraction of the circular region is encompassed by an angle of x degrees?

- $\frac{1}{36}$
- $\frac{1}{12}$
- $\frac{1}{9}$
- $\frac{1}{6}$
- The answer cannot be determined from the given information.

ANGLES AND FRACTIONS OF A CIRCLE

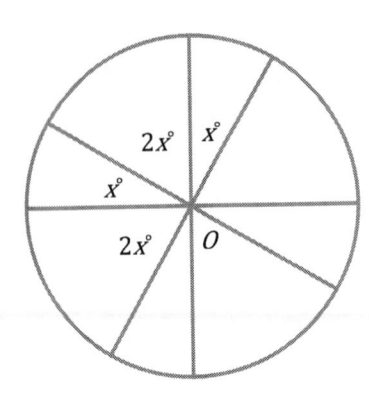

If O is the center of the circle above, what fraction of the circular region is encompassed by an angle of x degrees?

- $\frac{1}{36}$
- $\frac{1}{12}$
- $\frac{1}{9}$
- $\frac{1}{6}$
- The answer cannot be determined from the given information.

EXPLANATION

In this question, the angles shown appear span half the circle. We can infer that they must, in fact, because the opposite angles of bisecting lines are equal. On the other side of each of the $2x$ angles shown is another $2x$, and on the other side of each x shown is another x. Therefore,

$$2x + x + 2x + x = 180,$$

half the span of the circle. Thus, $6x = 180$ and $x = 30$. Since the full span of a circle is 360 degrees, the angle x spans a fraction of $\frac{30}{360} = \frac{1}{12}$.

The correct answer is (B).

What is the lowest positive integer that is divisible by every odd integer between 1 and 10?

- 105
- 315
- 945
- 3,780
- 7,560

Least Common Multiple

What is the lowest positive integer that is divisible by every odd integer between 1 and 10?

- 105
- 315
- 945
- 3,780
- 7,560

Explanation

"Every odd integer between 1 and 10" includes 1, 3, 5, 7, and 9. To be divisible by all of these numbers, it must have as factors at least one 5, one 7, and two 3's (two so that the 9 is covered). This minimum set of factors multiplies to $5 \times 7 \times 9 = 35 \times 9 = 270 + 45 = 315$. Therefore, the answer is (B).

A side note: since the factors of 315 happen to be prime numbers (with the 9 counted as two 3's), we have found the prime factorization of 315. Repeatedly dividing a number in order to get its prime factorization is a technique always to keep in mind when confronting confusing situations around multiplying, dividing, factors, and primes.

Again, the correct answer is (B).

If *n* is an integer, which of the following cannot be odd?

- $n + 2$
- $n + 3$
- $2n$
- $3n$
- n^2

CANNOT BE ODD

If *n* is an integer, which of the following cannot be odd?

- $n + 2$
- $n + 3$
- $2n$
- $3n$
- n^2

EXPLANATION

The mathematical definition of even and odd is that even numbers are divisible by 2, while odd numbers are not divisible by 2. Therefore, we can see that answer choice (C) cannot be odd. Dividing $2n$ by 2 will yield *n*, and we know *n* is an integer. Therefore, $2n$ cannot be odd.

An alternate way to solve this question is to analyze by cases. When looking at a specific answer choice, if you can pick a legal value of *n* so that it is odd, then it *can* be odd, and you know that it's not the correct answer to the question. In this fashion, you can eliminate all the answer choices other than (C). The correct answer is (C).

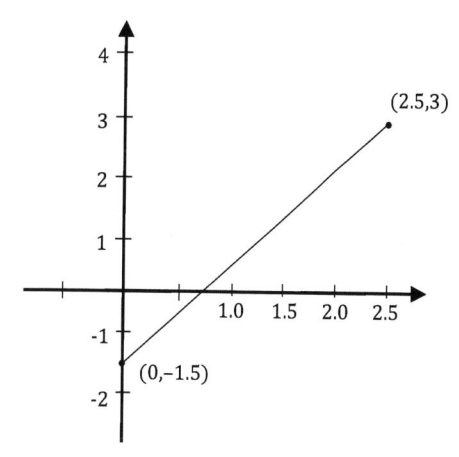

The point that bisects the line depicted in the figure above is

- (1.25,0.75)
- (1.25,2.25)
- (1.25,2)
- (1.25,1.25)
- (1.5,1.25)

Bisecting a Line

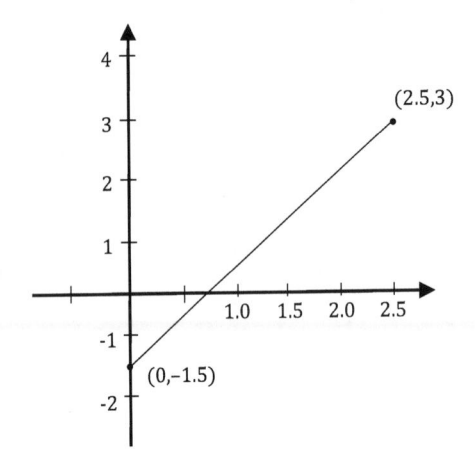

The point that bisects the line depicted in the figure above is

- (1.25, 0.75)
- (1.25, 2.25)
- (1.25, 2)
- (1.25, 1.25)
- (1.5, 1.25)

Explanation

The midpoint between any two points is found by averaging the two points' x-coordinates and their y-coordinates. (This can be proved from the Pythagorean Theorem, which also gives us the distance between two points in the coordinate plane.) The average of 2.5 and 0 is 1.25, so that is the x-coordinate of the midpoint. The average of 3 and -1.5 is $\frac{3+(-1.5)}{2} = \frac{1.5}{2} = 0.75$. The answer is (A).

Another approach here would be two find the equation of the line in the form $y = mx + b$. You can determine the slope m from the rise over run between the two points. The y-intercept b is -1.5. Then you could find the point on the line that is halfway along the run, at an x-value of 1.25, and you would find that at that x-value, $y = 0.75$.

Again, the correct answer is (A).

The sum $\frac{3}{8} + \frac{2}{9}$ is between

- 0 and $\frac{1}{2}$
- $\frac{1}{2}$ and $\frac{3}{4}$
- $\frac{3}{4}$ and 1
- 1 and $1\frac{1}{4}$
- $1\frac{1}{4}$ and $1\frac{1}{2}$

Estimating Sum of Fractions

The sum $\frac{3}{8} + \frac{2}{9}$ is between

- 0 and $\frac{1}{2}$
- $\frac{1}{2}$ and $\frac{3}{4}$
- $\frac{3}{4}$ and 1
- 1 and $1\frac{1}{4}$
- $1\frac{1}{4}$ and $1\frac{1}{2}$

Explanation

We could add these fractions either by finding a common denominator or by converting them into decimals. Both have easy-to-remember decimal conversions, we can use those. The fraction $\frac{3}{8}$ is a quarter plus a half of a quarter, so it's 0.375. The fraction $\frac{2}{9}$ is $\frac{2}{3}$ of $\frac{1}{3}$, which is $0.\overline{33}$, so it's $0.\overline{22}$. We'll call it 0.222, since the answer choices imply that an estimate will suffice. Adding the two, we get $0.375 + 0.222 = 0.597$. This is about 0.6, so it falls in the range described by (B). The correct answer is (B).

$1 - \left(\frac{2}{3} - \frac{3}{4}\right) =$

- $\frac{8}{7}$
- $\frac{13}{12}$
- $\frac{12}{13}$
- $\frac{7}{8}$
- 0

Fraction Subtraction

$1 - \left(\frac{2}{3} - \frac{3}{4}\right) =$

- $\frac{8}{7}$
- $\frac{13}{12}$
- $\frac{12}{13}$
- $\frac{7}{8}$
- 0

Explanation

To compare, add, or subtract fractions, we generally want a common denominator (unless we put them into decimal form). Here we can use a denominator of $3 \times 4 = 12$:

$$1 - \left(\frac{2}{3} - \frac{3}{4}\right) =$$

$$1 - \left(\frac{8}{12} - \frac{9}{12}\right) =$$

$$1 - \left(-\frac{1}{12}\right) =$$

$$\frac{13}{12}$$

The correct answer is (B).

If x is an integer, then the least possible value of $|100 - 7x|$ is

- 0
- 2
- 5
- 98
- 107

Possible Absolute Values

If x is an integer, then the least possible value of $|100 - 7x|$ is

- 0
- 2
- 5
- 98
- 107

Explanation

Insofar as this question talks about absolute value, we are dealing with the distance from zero. The 100 inside the bars essentially shifts that question so it's oriented not around zero, but how close $7x$ can get to 100, either above or below it. For example, if $x = 10$, then $7x = 70$, and the difference is 30. That's about four or five 7's further away then it could be. If $x = 15$, then $7x = 7(15) = 70 + 35 = 105$. That's a difference from 100 of 5, which I notice is an answer choice. But that can't be the least difference, because if we take off 7, we are at 98, just 2 off from 100. Those are the two closest multiples of 7.

The correct answer is (B).

Cyclist A averages 19.9 miles per hour and Cyclist B averages 15.1 miles per hour. If each cycle is ridden 1,500 miles, approximately how many more hours will Cyclist B ride than Cyclist A?

- 18
- 20
- 25
- 30
- 36

Difference in Distances over Time

Cyclist A averages 19.9 miles per hour and Cyclist B averages 15.1 miles per hour. If each cycle is ridden 1,500 miles, approximately how many more hours will Cyclist B ride than Cyclist A?

- 18
- 20
- 25
- 30
- 36

Explanation

This computation looks beastly, but the question says "approximately," so we can take the speed of A to be 20 miles per hour and that of B to be 15 miles per hour. (When we get to the stage of evaluating the answers, we'll recall that we approximated and question whether we have answered precisely enough.) Cyclist A rides at a constant rate of $\frac{20 \text{ miles}}{1 \text{ hour}}$. Without changing the rate, we want to get it to express the time for 1500 miles. To do this, we can multiply the fraction by 1:

$$\frac{20 \text{ miles}}{1 \text{ hour}} \times \frac{\frac{1500}{20}}{\frac{1500}{20}} = \frac{1500 \text{ miles}}{\frac{1500}{20} \text{ hours}}$$

So, A will take $\frac{1500}{20}$ hours. B will take $\frac{1500}{15}$ hours, which is more, because the denominator is smaller. It's easy enough to compute directly, but I would prefer to use the common denominator of 60:

$$\frac{1500}{15} - \frac{1500}{20}$$

$$\frac{4(1500)}{60} - \frac{3(1500)}{60}$$

$$\frac{1500}{60} = \frac{150}{6} = 25$$

Our estimate is 25.

The correct answer is (C).

If 5 is one solution of the equation $x^2 + 4x + m = 5$, where m is a constant, what is the other solution?

- −9
- −5
- −4
- 3
- 4

Other Solution of a Quadratic Equation

If 5 is one solution of the equation $x^2 + 4x + m = 5$, where m is a constant, what is the other solution?

- −9
- −5
- −4
- 3
- 4

Explanation

If 5 is a solution, then we can plug it in and find m:

$$25 + 20 + m = 5$$

Therefore, $m = -40$ and the equation is:

$$x^2 + 4x - 40 = 5$$

$$x^2 + 4x - 45 = 0$$

On the GMAT, when we get a quadratic equation, it can usually be solved by factoring. In this case:

$$(x+?)(x+?) = 0$$

The two question marks must add to +4 and multiply to −45, so we have

$$(x+9)(x-5) = 0$$

The two solutions are $x = -9$ and $x = 5$, and we already had 5. The correct answer is (A).

If $x = 1 - 4s$ and $y = 3s - 1$, then for what value of s does $x = y$?

- $\frac{7}{2}$
- $\frac{4}{3}$
- 1
- $\frac{2}{7}$
- 0

Two Equations Plus One Condition

If $x = 1 - 4s$ and $y = 3s - 1$, then for what value of s does $x = y$?

- $\frac{7}{2}$
- $\frac{4}{3}$
- 1
- $\frac{2}{7}$
- 0

Explanation

We want to know about the situation in which $x = y$, so we can set the thing that is x equal to the thing that is y:

$$1 - 4s = 3s - 1$$

$$2 - 4s = 3s$$

$$2 = 7s$$

$$s = \frac{2}{7}$$

The fraction is slightly awkward, but to confirm you could plug this value of s back into the original equation and note that $1 - 4\left(\frac{2}{7}\right) = -\frac{1}{7}$ and $3\left(\frac{2}{7}\right) - 1 = -\frac{1}{7}$.

The correct answer is (D).

How many integers *k* are there such that $1 < 7k - 14 < 49$?

- Seven
- Six
- Five
- Four
- Three

INTEGERS WITHIN AN INEQUALITY

How many integers k are there such that $1 < 7k - 14 < 49$?

- Seven
- Six
- Five
- Four
- Three

EXPLANATION

We can simplify the inequality by adding 14, to the left, center, and right:

$$1 < 7k - 14 < 49$$

$$15 < 7k < 63$$

Then we can divide left, center, and right by 7 to obtain:

$$\frac{15}{7} < k < 9$$

$$2\frac{1}{7} < k < 9$$

The possible values for k are 3, 4, 5, 6, 7, and 8. That's six integers.

The correct answer is (B).

The average (arithmetic mean) of 110, 30, and 85 is 10 less than the average of 40, 100, and

- 110
- 115
- 120
- 125
- 130

Comparing Two Averages

The average (arithmetic mean) of 110, 30, and 85 is 10 less than the average of 40, 100, and

- 110
- 115
- 120
- 125
- 130

Explanation

This question can be solved in various different ways that all boil down to the average formula. The average of the first three numbers is

$$\frac{110 + 30 + 85}{3} = \frac{140 + 85}{3} = \frac{225}{3} = 75$$

The average of the last three numbers is 10 higher, so it's 85. The differences of the three numbers from 85 must sum to zero. We have $40 - 85 = -45$ and $100 - 85 = 15$ so the net so far is -30, so the last number must be $85 + 30 = 115$. The correct answer is therefore (B).

Note: if you hadn't known about or didn't want to use the "differences" technique, you could have re-formed the average formula as $\frac{40+100+x}{3} = 85$ and solved for x, but I would contend that that method is slower for roughly 100% of people.

Again, the correct answer is (B).

Project	Number of men assigned to project	Number of women assigned to project	Total number of men and women assigned to project
1	a	b	200
2	a	c	180
3	b	c	70

In the table above, if no one is assigned to more than one project, what is the number of women assigned to Project 2?

- 100
- 75
- 50
- 25
- 15

Men and Women Assigned to Projects

Project	Number of men assigned to project	Number of women assigned to project	Total number of men and women assigned to project
1	a	b	200
2	a	c	180
3	b	c	70

In the table above, if no one is assigned to more than one project, what is the number of women assigned to Project 2?

- 100
- 75
- 50
- 25
- 15

Explanation

Since the rightmost column is a sum of the other two columns, the table gives us a series of equations:

$$a + b = 200$$

$$a + c = 180$$

$$b + c = 70$$

Although most people prefer solving by substitution, combination will be faster here. We can subtract the last equation from the first equation to get

$$a - c = 130$$

$$-a + c = -130$$

Adding this last equation to the second equation of the original set, we get

$$2c = 50$$

Therefore, $c = 25$.

The correct answer is (D).

The numbers of marbles of each of four different colors in a box are in the ratio 3 to 4 to 6 to 8. If there are 24 marbles of one of the colors, which of the following CANNOT be the total number of marbles in the box?

- 63
- 84
- 126
- 144
- 168

Ratios of Marbles

The numbers of marbles of each of four different colors in a box are in the ratio 3 to 4 to 6 to 8. If there are 24 marbles of one of the colors, which of the following CANNOT be the total number of marbles in the box?

- 63
- 84
- 126
- 144
- 168

Explanation

Since the ratio in this question has more than two elements, colon (or table) notation will be more useful than fraction notation:

A	B	C	D
$3n$	$4n$	$6n$	$8n$

The n conveys the fact that they are all multiples of some integer, but we don't know what integer; that's the definition of a ratio. The total of all the marbles is thus

$$3n + 4n + 6n + 8n = 21n$$

Most likely, the number that can't be the total, the correct answer choice, is not divisible by 21. Since $21 = 3 \times 7$, we can confirm by checking whether each is divisible by 7 and by 3.

The 3's are really easy, because we simply have to sum the digits and see whether the sum is divisible by 3. So we can do that first. $6 + 3 = 9$ divides by 3. $8 + 4 = 12$ divides by 3. $1 + 2 + 6 = 9$ divides by 3. $1 + 4 + 4 = 9$ divides by 3. $1 + 6 + 8 = 15$ divides by 3. All answer choices are still in.

On to 7. We have $63 = 7 \times 9$, $84 = 7 \times 12$, $126 = 7 \times 18$, $144 = 7 \times 2?$ ... 144 is not divisible by 7.

The correct answer is (D).

$\sqrt{45} + \sqrt{80} =$

- $7\sqrt{5}$
- $12\sqrt{5}$
- $25\sqrt{5}$
- $\sqrt{125}$
- 100

Summing Radicals

$\sqrt{45} + \sqrt{80} =$

- $7\sqrt{5}$
- $12\sqrt{5}$
- $25\sqrt{5}$
- $\sqrt{125}$
- 100

Explanation

As the answer choices make clear, we aren't calculating these square roots so much as reformatting them. The way to do that is to break the numbers inside into factors:

$$\sqrt{45} + \sqrt{80} =$$

$$\sqrt{9 \times 5} + \sqrt{5 \times 16} =$$

$$\sqrt{9}\sqrt{5} + \sqrt{5}\sqrt{16} =$$

$$3\sqrt{5} + 4\sqrt{5} = 7\sqrt{5}$$

The correct answer is (A).

A bucket collecting rainwater contained 15% more water in May than it had in April. If the bucket contained 345 cubic inches of water in May, how much water, in cubic inches, did it have in April?

- 293
- 300
- 308
- 317
- 334

Bucket of Rainwater

A bucket collecting rainwater contained 15% more water in May than it had in April. If the bucket contained 345 cubic inches of water in May, how much water, in cubic inches, did it have in April?

- 293
- 300
- 308
- 317
- 334

Explanation

If the amount in May is M and the amount in April is A, then the question tells us

$$M = 1.15A.$$

Then it tells us that $M = 345$, so we have

$$345 = 1.15A$$

$$A = \frac{345}{1.15}$$

I'm prepared to do long division if necessary, but since $300 = 3 \times 100$ and $45 = 3 \times 15$, $345 = 3 \times 115$. Then all we have to do is take the decimal point into consideration – although we can see the answer will be (B). 115 goes into 345 three times, so something a hundred times smaller goes in a hundred more times. Lastly, we can do a sanity check. This is April's number, and it should be smaller than May's. It is. Indeed, 15% of 300 is 10% plus half of 10%, so it's $30 + 15 = 45$.

The correct answer is (B).

A company's cash reserves held $10,000, and the reserves were spent and not replenished at a daily average of $1 each day over ten days. What percent of the original reserves was spent during this period?

- 0.0001%
- 0.001%
- 0.01%
- 0.1%
- 1%

Spending Cash Reserves

A company's cash reserves held $10,000, and the reserves were spent and not replenished at a daily average of $1 each day over ten days. What percent of the original reserves was spent during this period?

- 0.0001%
- 0.001%
- 0.01%
- 0.1%
- 1%

Explanation

This question is essentially asking, "What percent of $10,000 is $10?" Fair enough. Let's form a fraction:

$$\frac{10}{10,000}$$

$$= \frac{1}{1,000} = 10^{-3}$$

This is a fraction, not a percent. For the percent, we lose two decimal places, so it's 0.1%.

The correct answer is (D).

A solution contains 18 grams of active ingredient within every 100 cubic milliliters of solution. How many grams of active ingredient would be contained in a vessel of 40 cubic milliliters of the solution?

- 5.00
- 6.00
- 6.20
- 6.70
- 7.20

Volumes of a Solution

A solution contains 18 grams of active ingredient within every 100 cubic milliliters of solution. How many grams of active ingredient would be contained in a vessel of 40 cubic milliliters of the solution?

- 5.00
- 6.00
- 6.20
- 6.70
- 7.20

Explanation

If the phrasing of these solution questions ever confuses you, remember that they are just ratio questions, and that means we'll write fractions with unit labels. This solution can be written as follows:

$$\frac{18 \text{ g active ingredient}}{100 \text{ ml}^3}$$

Most people with a sense of efficiency wouldn't write the units so fully on their noteboards, but it's good to write something. We need to change the bottom of this ratio to 40 without changing the ratio, so we will multiply by 1:

$$\frac{18 \text{ g active ingredient}}{100 \text{ ml}^3} \times \frac{\frac{40}{100}}{\frac{40}{100}}$$

$$\frac{18 \times \frac{40}{100} \text{ g active ingredient}}{40 \text{ ml}^3}$$

$$\frac{18 \times \frac{2}{5} \text{ g active ingredient}}{40 \text{ ml}^3}$$

Then, $18 \times \frac{2}{5} = \frac{36}{5} = 7\frac{1}{5} = 7.2$. We can do a sanity check: the solution has dropped by more than half. So has our amount of active ingredient.

The correct answer is (E).

$$y = mx - 3$$

In the equation above, *m* is a constant. If $y = 33$ when $x = 6$, what is the value of y when $x = 12$?

- 69
- 66
- 63
- 60
- 33

EQUATION OF A LINE

$$y = mx - 3$$

In the equation above, m is a constant. If $y = 33$ when $x = 6$, what is the value of y when $x = 12$?

- 69
- 66
- 63
- 60
- 33

EXPLANATION

In this question, the purpose of the first pair of x-y values is to allow us to solve for m. Then we can use the complete equation to solve for what is asked. So, step 1, to get m, we substitute into the equation:

$$33 = m(6) - 3$$

$$36 = m(6)$$

$$m = 6$$

Then we use m and the value of x we are given:

$$y = (6)(12) - 3$$

$$y = 72 - 3 = 69$$

To check your answer, you could note that the equation is for a line with a slope of 6 and a downward offset of 3. That fits with both the first pair and second pair of coordinates.

The correct answer is (A).

In the *xy*-plane, what is the slope of the line with equation $4x + 5y = 6$?

- ○ $-\dfrac{5}{4}$
- ○ $-\dfrac{4}{5}$
- ○ $\dfrac{4}{5}$
- ○ 4
- ○ 5

Slope of a Line

In the *xy*-plane, what is the slope of the line with equation $4x + 5y = 6$?

- ○ $-\frac{5}{4}$
- ○ $-\frac{4}{5}$
- ○ $\frac{4}{5}$
- ○ 4
- ○ 5

Explanation

The easiest way to find the slope of this line is to convert the equation into the form $y = mx + b$, and in that case the value of m will be the slope. This process amounts to isolating y by applying operations to both sides of the equation.

$$4x + 5y = 6$$

$$5y = -4x + 6$$

$$y = -\frac{4}{5}x + \frac{6}{5}$$

The slope is $-\frac{4}{5}$.

The correct answer is (B).

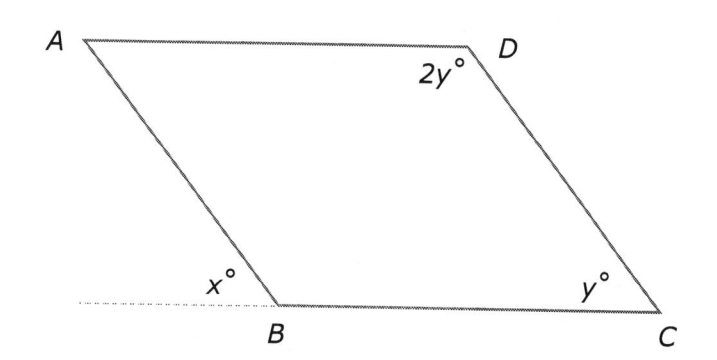

In the figure above, if ABCD is a parallelogram, then x =

- 30
- 40
- 60
- 90
- 180

Angles of a Parallelogram

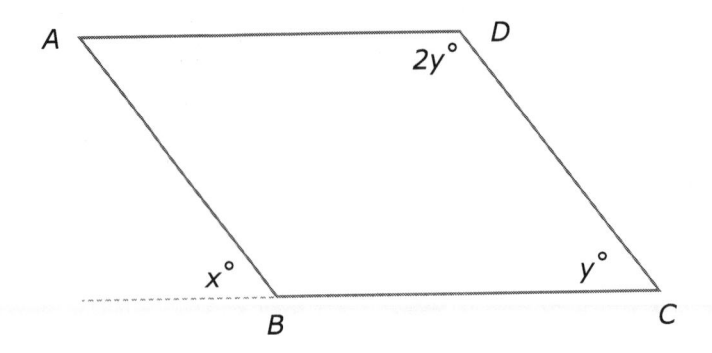

In the figure above, if *ABCD* is a parallelogram, then *x* =

- 30
- 40
- 60
- 90
- 180

Explanation

Since *ABCD* is a parallelogram, facing angles are equal, as they in fact appear to be. And all of the angles add up to 90 times the number of angles:

$$y + 2y + y + 2y = 360$$

$$6y = 360$$

$$y = 60$$

Meanwhile, *x* and the angle next to it, 2*y*, are complementary to the full measure of a line, which is 180 degrees. Therefore,

$$x + 2y = 180$$

$$x + 120 = 180$$

$$x = 60$$

The correct answer is (C).

Pat bought both carrots and onions from a store. If each carrot cost $1.10, each onion cost $0.50, and the purchase of carrots and onions totaled $11.00, what total number of carrots and onions did Pat buy?

- 10
- 11
- 12
- 13
- 16

Carrots and Onions Purchased

Pat bought both carrots and onions from a store. If each carrot cost $1.10, each onion cost $0.50, and the purchase of carrots and onions totaled $11.00, what total number of carrots and onions did Pat buy?

- 10
- 11
- 12
- 13
- 16

Explanation

In this question, if we call the number of carrots bought C, and the number of onions bought N (so as not to confuse ourselves with zero), then we have

$$1.1C + 0.5N = 11$$

That might not seem like enough to solve, but we know that Pat bought at least one of each. So we can't have $C = 10, N = 0$ or $C = 0, N = 22$. The fact that both C and N are integers also limits the possibilities. Since C is larger, we can start there and see how it contributes, in various cases to the total of 11. You could write, or partly write and imagine the following table:

$$C = 1 \to \$1.10$$

$$C = 2 \to \$2.20$$

$$C = 3 \to \$3.30$$

$$C = 4 \to \$4.40$$

$$C = 5 \to \$5.50$$

This last case is special. Since we have at least one carrot and at least on onion, we need some multiple of their prices to add to eleven dollars. This is the first possibility we've found, since we can't have $C = 10, N = 0$ or $C = 0, N = 22$. In this case, the number of carrots is 5. The remaining amount of dollars is $5.50, which amounts to 11 onions. The total number of vegetable items purchased is 11+5=16.

The correct answer is (E).

On Wednesday, a restaurant sold a quantity of wine in 6 ounce servings, and on Thursday, it sold the same total quantity of wine in 4 ounce servings. If the price on Wednesday was $9.00 per glass, and the revenue on Thursday was $\frac{3}{4}$ that of the revenue on Wednesday, what was the price per glass of the wine on Thursday?

- $4.00
- $4.50
- $6.00
- $6.75
- $10.13

Serving Size, Price and Revenue

On Wednesday, a restaurant sold a quantity of wine in 6 ounce servings, and on Thursday, it sold the same total quantity of wine in 4 ounce servings. If the price on Wednesday was $9.00 per glass, and the revenue on Thursday was $\frac{3}{4}$ that of the revenue on Wednesday, what was the price per glass of the wine on Thursday?

- $4.00
- $4.50
- $6.00
- $6.75
- $10.13

Explanation

A lot of pieces of information are floating around in this question: revenue, glasses, prices. We can relate them in that revenue will be the number of glasses times the price:

$$\text{revenue} = (\text{number of glasses})(\text{price})$$

And we have a relationship between the revenue on the two days:

$$(\text{number of glasses on W})(\text{price on W})\left(\frac{3}{4}\right) = (\text{number of glasses on Th})(\text{price on Th})$$

Putting in the fact that the price on Wednesday was $9, and isolating the price on Thursday, we get:

$$(\text{price on Th}) = \frac{(\text{number of glasses on W})}{(\text{number of glasses on Th})} (9) \left(\frac{3}{4}\right)$$

We have information to determine the number of glasses. Consider the case in which 24 ounces of wine was sold. The number of glasses would be 4 on Wednesday and 6 on Thursday, so the ratio of glasses sold is 2 to 3:

$$(\text{price on Th}) = \left(\frac{2}{3}\right)(9)\left(\frac{3}{4}\right) = \frac{9}{2} = 4.5$$

That indicates a price per glass on Thursday of $4.50.

We can double-check that this makes sense: if the number of glasses sold was 50% higher on Thursday, but the revenue was only 75%, then the price per glass would have to be much lower. Continuing with the case we discussed, if on Wednesday the number of glasses was 4, then the revenue would be $4 \times 9 = 36$. And the revenue on Wednesday would be $\left(\frac{3}{4}\right)36 = 27$ for 6 glasses, so the price must be $4.50. Indeed, we could have solved the question this way straightaway. The correct answer is (B).

If 1 foot is approximately 0.3 meters, which of the following best approximates the number of feet in 5 meters?

- $\frac{50}{3}$
- 15
- 1.5
- $\frac{1}{15}$
- $\frac{3}{50}$

CONVERTING UNITS

If 1 foot is approximately 0.3 meters, which of the following best approximates the number of feet in 5 meters?

- ○ $\frac{50}{3}$
- ○ 15
- ○ 1.5
- ○ $\frac{1}{15}$
- ○ $\frac{3}{50}$

EXPLANATION

We can use fraction terminology here. We are given a fixed ratio:

$$\frac{1 \text{ foot}}{0.3 \text{ meters}}$$

To get 5 meters without altering the ratio, we can multiply by 1:

$$= \frac{1 \text{ foot}}{0.3 \text{ meters}} \times \frac{\frac{5}{0.3}}{\frac{5}{0.3}}$$

$$= \frac{\frac{5}{0.3} \text{ foot}}{5 \text{ meters}}$$

The loads of fractions may seem laborious, but they prevent error, and by being quite organized, you can move quickly with complete confidence. Anyway, the number of feet corresponding to 5 meters is $\frac{5}{0.3}$. We can switch to fractions:

$$\frac{5}{0.3} = \frac{5}{\frac{3}{10}} \times \frac{\frac{10}{3}}{\frac{10}{3}} = \frac{50}{3}$$

We have our answer. An alternative way to set up the calculation which is mathematically identical is to write

$$\frac{1 \text{ foot}}{0.3 \text{ meters}} = \frac{x \text{ feet}}{5 \text{ meters}}$$

and then solve for x by cross-multiplying. The correct answer is (A).

If k is the average (arithmetic mean) of the first 8 positive multiples of 6 greater than 6, and if p is the median of the first 8 positive multiples of 6 greater than 6, what is the value of $\frac{k}{p}$?

- $\frac{10}{11}$
- 1
- $\frac{11}{10}$
- $\frac{12}{11}$
- 0

Comparing Mean and Median

If *k* is the average (arithmetic mean) of the first 8 positive multiples of 6 greater than 6, and if *p* is the median of the first 8 positive multiples of 6 greater than 6, what is the value of $\frac{k}{p}$?

- $\frac{10}{11}$
- 1
- $\frac{11}{10}$
- $\frac{12}{11}$
- 0

Explanation

We can exhaustively enumerate what we are talking about here: the first 8 positive multiples of 6 greater than 6 are: {12, 18, 24, 30, 36, 42, 48, 54}. Their median is the average of the middle two, so it's 33. And moving out from 30 and 36, the numbers are evenly spaced from 33 in pairs. For example, 54 − 33 = 21, and 33 − 12 = 21, so the first and the last cancel in pulling the average "left" or "right" of 33. Therefore, the median and the mean are both 33, and the ratio of one to the other is 1.

The correct answer is (B).

The number of visible stars in the night sky, T, can be estimated by the formula

$$T = \left(\frac{4\pi L^2}{A}\right) N,$$

where N is the number of stars counted through a tube with length L, in centimeters, a mouth of area A, in square centimeters. Based on the formula, what is the estimated number of visible stars in the night sky if 240 stars are observed through a tube 10 feet long with a mouth of radius of 4 feet? (1 foot = 30.48 centimeters)

- 182,880
- 7,000
- 6,000
- 5,800
- 500

Visible Stars in the Night Sky

The number of visible stars in the night sky, T, can be estimated by the formula

$$T = \left(\frac{4\pi L^2}{A}\right) N,$$

where N is the number of stars counted through a tube with length L, in centimeters, a mouth of area A, in square centimeters. Based on the formula, what is the estimated number of visible stars in the night sky if 240 stars are observed through a tube 10 feet long with a mouth of radius of 4 feet? (1 foot = 30.48 centimeters)

- 182,880
- 7,000
- 6,000
- 5,800
- 500

Explanation

This question boils down to careful plugging. First, we need to get L and the radius in the right units:

$$L = 10 \text{ feet} = 10 \text{ feet} \times \frac{30.48 \text{ cm}}{1 \text{ feet}} = 304.8 \text{ cm}$$

$$r = 4 \text{ feet} = 4 \text{ feet} \times \frac{30.48 \text{ cm}}{1 \text{ feet}} = 4(30.48) \text{ cm}$$

We can calculate the area A from the radius. Let's not be too eager to multiply those numbers, however:

$$A = \pi r^2 = \pi\big(4(30.48)\big)^2.$$

Now, we plug everything into the main formula and simplify as much as possible before computing:

$$T = \left(\frac{4\pi(304.8)^2}{\pi\big(4(30.48)\big)^2}\right)240 = \left(\frac{4\pi(304.8)^2}{\pi 4^2(30.48)^2}\right)240$$

$$T = \left(\frac{(304.8)^2}{4(30.48)^2}\right)240$$

$$T = \left(\frac{(30.48 \times 10)^2}{4(30.48)^2}\right)240$$

$$T = \left(\frac{10^2}{4}\right)240 = 100 \times 60 = 6,000$$

The correct answer is (C).

In the coordinate plane, a circle has center (−1, −3) and passes through the point (4,2). What is the circumference of the circle?

- $5\sqrt{2}\pi$
- $10\sqrt{2}\pi$
- $10\sqrt{3}\pi$
- 25π
- 50π

Circle in the Coordinate Plane

In the coordinate plane, a circle has center (−1, −3) and passes through the point (4,2). What is the circumference of the circle?

- $5\sqrt{2}\pi$
- $10\sqrt{2}\pi$
- $10\sqrt{3}\pi$
- 25π
- 50π

Explanation

To find the circumference of this circle, we need its radius. And the radius is the distance from its center to any point on the circle, so the radius is the distance from (−1,−3) to (4,2).

This distance is computed with the distance formula, which is essentially the Pythagorean Theorem. The sides of the triangle are the x and y distances, 5 and 5, so the distance is $\sqrt{5^2 + 5^2} = \sqrt{25 + 25} = \sqrt{2(25)} = 5\sqrt{2}$. The radius of the circle is $5\sqrt{2}$, so the circumference is $2\pi r = 2\pi(5\sqrt{2}) = 10\sqrt{2}\pi$.

The correct answer is (B).

The average distance between the Earth and the moon is approximately 3.8×10^5 kilometers. Which of the following is the closest to the average distance in feet? (1 kilometer is approximately 3.2×10^4 feet.)

- 7.0×10^9
- 1.1×10^{10}
- 1.2×10^{10}
- 1.2×10^{11}
- 9.9×10^{11}

Distance to the Moon

The average distance between the Earth and the moon is approximately 3.8×10^5 kilometers. Which of the following is the closest to the average distance in feet? (1 kilometer is approximately 3.2×10^4 feet.)

- 7.0×10^9
- 1.1×10^{10}
- 1.2×10^{10}
- 1.2×10^{11}
- 9.9×10^{11}

Explanation

In this question, we can use dimensional analysis, the practice of writing and multiplying fractions such that units cancel as desired:

$$(3.8 \times 10^5 \text{ km}) \times \left(\frac{3.2 \times 10^4 \text{ feet}}{1 \text{ km}}\right)$$

Writing the units makes it easy to determine whether we are multiplying or dividing the quantities. We can drop the units now, since we'll be working in feet from this point forward.

$$3.8 \times 10^5 \times 3.2 \times 10^4$$

$$(3.8 \times 3.2) \times 10^9$$

There are many approaches to making this calculation easier. One approach is to ignore the decimals at first and observe that we have almost forty 32's; since it's thirty-eight 32's, it's forty 32's minus two 32's, or 64. But the bottom line is that it's good to reserve some space on the side of your notebook for when you have to do some multiplying or dividing that warrants writing.

$$12.16 \times 10^9$$

$$1.216 \times 10^{10}$$

The correct answer is (C).

S = {2, 3, 4, 6}

T = {2, 3, 4, 6}

Two integers will be randomly selected from the sets above, one integer from set S and one integer from set T. What is the probability that the product of the two integers will equal 12?

- 0.20
- $\frac{3}{16}$
- 0.25
- 0.30
- $\frac{1}{3}$

Probability of Pairs of Draws

$$S = \{2, 3, 4, 6\}$$

$$T = \{2, 3, 4, 6\}$$

Two integers will be randomly selected from the sets above, one integer from set S and one integer from set T. What is the probability that the product of the two integers will equal 12?

- 0.20
- $\frac{3}{16}$
- 0.25
- 0.30
- $\frac{1}{3}$

Explanation

In this question, we can start with the draw from Set S and imagine the case in which the draw is a 2. In this case, the product of the S draw and the T draw will be 12 only if the T draw is 6, and there is a $\frac{1}{4}$ possibility of that T draw. Imagining another case, if the S draw is 3, the T draw must be 4. Again, a $\frac{1}{4}$ possibility. Indeed, the probability is $\frac{1}{4}$ in any case, so the correct answer is (C).

Consider this variation: What if there's no set T at all, and we want to know the probabilities if there are two *distinct* draws from Set S? If the draws must be distinct, then in the case in which we draw a 2, there are only three numbers left, so the probability of drawing a 6 is $\frac{1}{3}$. The probability is $\frac{1}{3}$ in all cases and is the answer to that variation on the question.

Another variation: What if set T has a 5 rather than a 6? Then the probability is not the same in all cases: it's zero if we draw a 2 from set S, and it's $\frac{1}{4}$ in the other cases. The expected value in this variation is $(0)\frac{1}{4} + \left(\frac{1}{4}\right)\frac{1}{4} + \left(\frac{1}{4}\right)\frac{1}{4} + \left(\frac{1}{4}\right)\frac{1}{4} = \frac{3}{16}$.

Again, in this question, the correct answer is (C).

At a certain school, the ratio of the number of five-year-old's to the number of nine-year-old's is 12 to 5, and the ratio of the number of four-year-old's to the number of five-year old's is 3 to 4. If the ratio of the number of eight-year-old's to the number of nine-year-old's is 3 to 2, what is the ratio of the number of four-year-old's to the number of eight-year-old's?

- 24 to 23
- 11 to 6
- 3 to 2
- 6 to 5
- 5 to 6

RATIOS OF CHILDREN

At a certain school, the ratio of the number of five-year-old's to the number of nine-year-old's is 12 to 5, and the ratio of the number of four-year-old's to the number of five-year old's is 3 to 4. If the ratio of the number of eight-year-old's to the number of nine-year-old's is 3 to 2, what is the ratio of the number of four-year-old's to the number of eight-year-old's?

- 24 to 23
- 11 to 6
- 3 to 2
- 6 to 5
- 5 to 6

EXPLANATION

Since we have more than two parts in the overall ratio here, a table is useful:

4yo	5yo	8yo	9yo
	12		5
3	4		
		3	2

The various two-part relationships are written on different rows because they have not yet been related to each other. We can relate them through multiples. For example, by tripling the 4 in the second row and comparing with the first row, we can see that the top-left-most entry should be 9.

To combine the first row and the third row, we need to relate them based on the last column, which we can do by converting both into the common multiple of 10. We can write the multiple of the first row as a new row and fill in the missing multiple from the third row:

4yo	5yo	8yo	9yo	
9	12		5	(x2)
3	4			
		3	2	(x5)
18	24	15	10	

Therefore, the ratio of four-year-old's to eight-year-old's is 18 to 15, or $\frac{18}{3} = 6$ to $\frac{15}{3} = 5$.

The correct answer is (D).

If $x\left(\frac{5n+1}{3}\right) = x$ and $x \neq 0$, then $n =$

- $\frac{1}{5}$
- $\frac{3}{5}$
- $\frac{2}{5}$
- 1
- 5

Needless Variable

If $x\left(\frac{5n+1}{3}\right) = x$ and $x \neq 0$, then $n =$

- $\frac{1}{5}$
- $\frac{3}{5}$
- $\frac{2}{5}$
- 1
- 5

Explanation

This question is a bit silly because it gives us x's that we can get rid of by dividing both sides of the equation by x:

$$\frac{5n+1}{3} = 1$$

$$5n + 1 = 3$$

$$5n = 2$$

$$n = \frac{2}{5}$$

The correct answer is (C).

The number of cars present at a particular time was measured at 3,999 different locations on Tuesday and on Wednesday. The number of locations that had more cars on Wednesday was 15% higher than the number of locations that had more cars on Tuesday. How many of the locations had more cars on Tuesday?

- 1,159
- 1,333
- 1,860
- 2,460
- 2,829

Comparing Car Counts at a Location

The number of cars present at a particular time was measured at 3,999 different locations on Tuesday and on Wednesday. The number of locations that had more cars on Wednesday was 15% higher than the number of locations that had more cars on Tuesday. How many of the locations had more cars on Tuesday?

- 1,159
- 1,333
- 1,860
- 2,460
- 2,829

Explanation

The question states that all these 3,999 locations were measured twice, once on each day. It also breaks the 3,999 into two groups, the higher-on-Tuesday locations and the higher-on-Wednesday locations, which we can call T and W. Therefore, we can write two equations:

$$T + W = 3{,}999$$

$$W = 1.15T$$

Substituting the second equation into the first one, we have

$$T + 1.15T = 3{,}999$$

$$2.15T = 3{,}999$$

$$T = \frac{3{,}999}{2.15}$$

If we do just two places of the long division, we can narrow the answer choices to one:

```
              1  8.  6
       ┌─────────────────
   215 │ 3  9  9  9.  0
         2  1  5
         ─────────
         1  8  4  9
         1  7  2  0
         ─────────
            1  2  9  0
            1  2  9  0
            ─────────
                     0
```

The correct answer is (C).

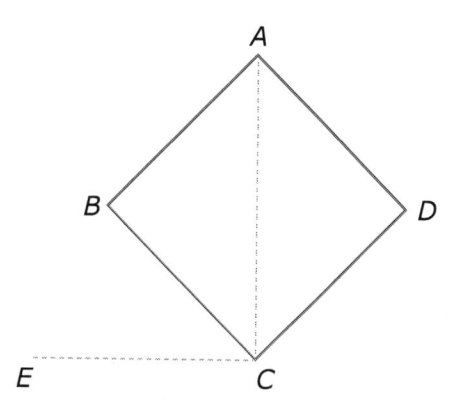

In the figure above, AC passes through the center of the square ABCD, and CE is perpendicular to AC. What is the minimum number of degrees the square must be rotated so that BC will be parallel to EC?

- 45
- 90
- 135
- 180
- 270

Rotating a Square

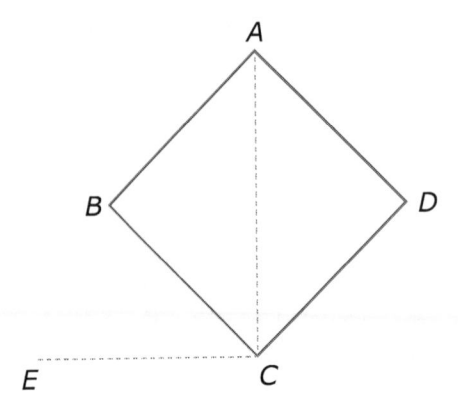

[Figure: Square ABCD rotated so that A is at top, B at left, D at right, C at bottom. A dashed line runs from A through the center to C, and a dashed line extends horizontally from C to E on the left.]

In the figure above, AC passes through the center of the square ABCD, and CE is perpendicular to AC. What is the minimum number of degrees the square must be rotated so that BC will be parallel to EC?

- 45
- 90
- 135
- 180
- 270

Explanation

In this question, if this square were a handle or a doorknob, we would be grabbing it and turning it left or counter-clockwise just a bit, until the side *BC* comes to rest along the line segment *EC*, which we imagine has not rotated. But how much? The angle *ACE* is a right angle, so its degree measure is 90. Meanwhile, the angle *ACB* must be 45, because the line *AC* bisects the angle *BCD*. We can conclude that the side *BC* bisects the right angle of the dotted line and must be turned 45 degrees to reach *EC*.

The correct answer is (A).

If $z + 7 > 2$ and $z - 3 < 5$, then which of the following must be true?

- $-6 < z < 8$
- $-5 < z < 2$
- $2 < z < 5$
- $4 < z < 5$
- $5 < z < 8$

Combining Inequalities

If $z + 7 > 2$ and $z - 3 < 5$, then which of the following must be true?

- $-6 < z < 8$
- $-5 < z < 2$
- $2 < z < 5$
- $4 < z < 5$
- $5 < z < 8$

Explanation

Both of these inequalities can be simplified. Generally, you can treat inequalities like equations in the sense that you can do something to one if you do it to the other. (The exception, which doesn't apply here, is that if you multiply or divide both sides by a negative number, you must flip the direction of the inequality.) From $z + 7 > 2$ we have $z > -5$, and $z - 3 < 5$ gives $z < 8$. Combining them, we have $-5 < z < 8$. That's not in the answer choices – have we made a mistake? Not necessarily. We can consider possible cases. If $-5 < z < 8$, then a possible value of z is zero. That means that it's not true that (C) must be true, or (D), or (E), so we can rule them out. Similarly, if $-5 < z < 8$, z could be 7, or 7.5 So (B) need not be true. *Must* (A) be true? Indeed, it must. If z is right of -5 on the number line, then it's always going to be right of -6 on the number line.

The correct answer is (A).

A total number of paperclips can be divided into 24 smaller piles of an equal number of clips each or 30 smaller piles of an equal number of clips each. What is the lowest possible total number of paperclips?

- 30
- 60
- 120
- 180
- 720

Divisibility into Paperclip Piles

A total number of paperclips can be divided into 24 smaller piles of an equal number of clips each or 30 smaller piles of an equal number of clips each. What is the lowest possible total number of paperclips?

- 30
- 60
- 120
- 180
- 720

Explanation

The total number of paperclips is divisible by 24 and by 30. To find the smallest such number, we can find the prime factorizations of 24 and 30, by dividing them into factors until we can divide no further. We have $24 = 2^3 \times 3$ and $30 = 2 \times 3 \times 5$. Our total number must therefore have at least three 2's, one 3, and one 5. The smallest possibility is $2^3 \times 3 \times 5 = 40 \times 3 = 120$.

The correct answer is (C).

A company's profits obtained from Product A, Product B, and Product C are in the ratio 47:1:2, respectively. If the total profits from these three products is $16,000, what is the profit from Product C?

- $1,610
- $1,290
- $960
- $640
- $320

Ratio of Profits

A company's profits obtained from Product A, Product B, and Product C are in the ratio 47:1:2, respectively. If the total profits from these three products is $16,000, what is the profit from Product C?

- $1,610
- $1,290
- $960
- $640
- $320

Explanation

Ratios can be thought of as containing an unknown that represents in the multiple of the ratio. So, since these profits are in the ratio of 47:1:2, we can represent their total profit as $47n + n + 2n$, where n is an integer. That means that $50n = 16,000$, so $n = \frac{16,000}{50} = \frac{1,600}{5} = 320$. We are looking for the profit from Product C, and that's $2n = 2(320) = 640$.

The correct answer is (D).

If three sides of a rectangular solid have areas of 12, 18, and 24, what is the volume of the solid?

- 72
- 144
- 576
- 2,592
- 5,184

Volume from Area

If three sides of a rectangular solid have areas of 12, 18, and 24, what is the volume of the solid?

- 72
- 144
- 576
- 2,592
- 5,184

Explanation

If we call the dimensions of this rectangular solid are a, b, and c, then its volume will be abc. Also, we know that $ab = 12$, $bc = 18$, and $ac = 24$. We could solve properly through substitution, but we can also directly get the values of these by looking at the factors:

$$ab = 12 = 3 \times 4$$

$$bc = 18 = 3 \times 6$$

$$ac = 24 = 4 \times 6$$

Looking at which factors are common to which variable pairs, we must have $a = 4$, $b = 3$, $c = 6$. Therefore, the volume is $3 \times 4 \times 6 = 12 \times 6 = 72$.

The correct answer is (A).

At 3:00 pm, a car has driven 30 miles east. It will continue to drive east at 0.8 minutes per mile and then turn around and drive at 0.8 minutes per mile back to its original starting point. How far can it drive before turning around in order to arrive back to its original starting point by 3:40 pm?

- 10
- 11
- 12
- 13
- 14

Time to Turn Around

At 3:00 pm, a car has driven 30 miles east. It will continue to drive east at 0.8 minutes per mile and then turn around and drive at 0.8 minutes per mile back to its original starting point. How far can it drive before turning around in order to arrive back to its original starting point by 3:40 pm?

- 10
- 11
- 12
- 13
- 14

Explanation

The constant speed of this car can be written as $\frac{0.8 \text{ minutes}}{1 \text{ mile}}$. Since this rate doesn't change in the question, we will solve by setting this equal to an equivalent fraction:

$$\frac{0.8 \text{ minutes}}{1 \text{ mile}} = \frac{? \text{ minutes}}{? \text{ miles}}$$

The question is what goes in the place of the question marks. Since the numerator is minutes, that will be 40 minutes, the time from 3:00 pm to 3:40 pm. To determine the distance, we could draw a little diagram:

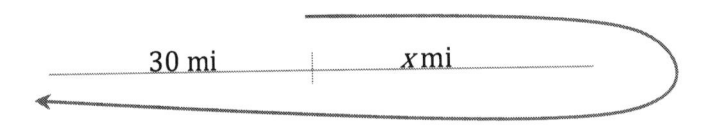

```
    30 mi    |    x mi
<-----------------------\
                         )
                        /
```

This diagram is a schematic and not exact, in the sense that the car is actually going straight along the line and then turning around and going right back along the straight line, not along a curve. The curve is how we can sketch it to understand going x miles, turning around, and going x miles back. The total distance is $x + x + 30$ miles. Plugging in, we have

$$\frac{0.8 \text{ minutes}}{1 \text{ mile}} = \frac{40 \text{ minutes}}{2x + 30 \text{ miles}}$$

Cross-multiplying gives

$$1.6x + 24 = 40$$

$$1.6x = 16$$

So, $x=10$. Let's confirm this is what we are looking for, checking the sketch we made. We've found the distance the car can go before it has to turn around. That's right.

The correct answer is (A).

At least $\frac{3}{4}$ of the 50 players on a sports team must receive an award individually from the state in order for the team as a whole to receive an award from the state. What is the greatest number of team members that could fail to receive an award individually from the state, if the team as a whole receives an award from the state?

- 15
- 14
- 13
- 12
- 11

TEAM AWARD

At least $\frac{3}{4}$ of the 50 players on a sports team must receive an award individually from the state in order for the team as a whole to receive an award from the state. What is the greatest number of team members that could fail to receive an award individually from the state, if the team as a whole receives an award from the state?

- 15
- 14
- 13
- 12
- 11

EXPLANATION

At least $\frac{3}{4}$ members of these 50 team members need to win an award, so the number who win an award must be at least $\frac{3}{4} \times 50 = \frac{3}{2} \times 25 = 37.5$.

These people and their awards come only in whole numbers, so that means that 38 people must win, since 37 < 37.5 and would fail to meet the condition. Since at least 38 of 50 must get the award, at most 12 of 50 don't get the award.

The correct answer is (D).

If $x = 100! + 11$, then x must be divisible by which of the following?

- 11
- 89
- 100
- 111
- 121

Divisibility of a Large Number

If $x = 100! + 11$, then x must be divisible by which of the following?

- o 11
- o 89
- o 100
- o 111
- o 121

Explanation

This question uses factorial notation. $100! = 100 \times 99 \times 98 \ldots$, all the way down to 1. So x is that large product plus 11. Let's consider the simplest case from the answer choices, x divided by 11:

$$\frac{x}{11} = \frac{100! + 11}{11}$$

If this thing is an integer, than x is divisible by 11. It's equal to

$$\frac{100!}{11} + \frac{11}{11}$$

The second term here becomes one. The first one is an integer. In fact, 100! is divisible by every integer from 1 to 100, because it contains all of them as a factor. So $\frac{x}{11} = \frac{100!+11}{11}$ is an integer, and x is divisible by 11. Similar logic shows that the other answer choices do not yield integers.

The correct answer is (A).

$$\frac{(0.00024)(1.6)}{(0.01)(0.04)(0.003)} =$$

- 320.0
- 32.0
- 3.2
- 0.32
- 0.032

Fraction of Many Decimals

$$\frac{(0.00024)(1.6)}{(0.01)(0.04)(0.003)} =$$

- 320.0
- 32.0
- 3.2
- 0.32
- 0.032

Explanation

In this question, as in general, we will try to cancel as much as possible before doing any substantial computation. First, we can put all the terms in scientific notation and do a roundup of the powers of ten:

$$\frac{(2.4 \times 10^{-4})(1.6)}{(1 \times 10^{-2})(4 \times 10^{-2})(3 \times 10^{-3})}$$

$$= \frac{(2.4)(1.6)}{(1)(4)(3)} \times \frac{10^{-4}}{10^{-7}}$$

Meanwhile, $\frac{10^{-4}}{10^{-7}}$ cancels partly to yield $\frac{1}{10^{-3}}$, which is $\frac{1}{\frac{1}{10^3}}$ or 10^3. So we are favoring answer choice (A) at this point, based on that basic order of magnitude. In the left factor, we can cancel the 4 partly with the 1.6 and the 3 with the 2.4 to get:

$$= (0.8)(0.4) \times 10^3 = 0.32 \times 10^3 = 320.$$

The correct answer is (A).

If $x = \frac{1}{10} + \frac{1}{12} + \frac{1}{13} + \frac{1}{14} + \frac{1}{15}$, which of the following is true?

- $\frac{7}{15} > x > \frac{1}{2}$
- $\frac{1}{2} > x > \frac{1}{3}$
- $\frac{1}{3} > x > \frac{1}{5}$
- $\frac{1}{5} > x > \frac{1}{7}$
- $\frac{1}{7} > x > \frac{1}{9}$

Estimating a Sum of Many Fractions

If $x = \frac{1}{10} + \frac{1}{12} + \frac{1}{13} + \frac{1}{14} + \frac{1}{15}$, which of the following is true?

- $\frac{7}{15} > x > \frac{1}{2}$
- $\frac{1}{2} > x > \frac{1}{3}$
- $\frac{1}{3} > x > \frac{1}{5}$
- $\frac{1}{5} > x > \frac{1}{7}$
- $\frac{1}{7} > x > \frac{1}{9}$

Explanation

In this question, x is a sum of fractions. The first one, $\frac{1}{10}$, is the largest one, because it has the smallest denominator, and the last one, $\frac{1}{15}$, is the smallest of the terms, since it has the largest denominator. Since $\frac{1}{10}$ is the largest of these 5 terms, we know they will be less than $5 \times \frac{1}{10} = \frac{1}{2}$. And since $\frac{1}{15}$ is the smallest of the five terms, we know they will be greater than $5 \times \frac{1}{15} = \frac{1}{3}$. Therefore, $\frac{1}{3} < x < \frac{1}{2}$.

The correct answer is (B).

What was the approximate total amount of interest paid on a 2-year, $1,000 note that pays interest at an annual rate of 6 percent compounded semiannually?

- $120
- $113
- $108
- $106
- $101

Compound Interest

What was the approximate total amount of interest paid on a 2-year, $1,000 note that pays interest at an annual rate of 6 percent compounded semiannually?

- $120
- $113
- $108
- $106
- $101

Explanation

In question, the phrase "annual rate of 6 percent compounded semiannually" means that, in half a year, the investment value increases by 3%. So, after the first six months, the $1,000 is worth 1,000(1.03). Since this is compound interest and not simple interest, over the next six months, *that* value – the 1,000(1.03) and not just the original 1,000 – increases at the same rate, so at the end of that period, we have 1,000(1.03)(1.03). At the end of two years, four "compoundings," we have a total value of

$$\$1,000(1.03)^4$$

First, we can calculate $(1.03)^2 = 1.0609$. That means that, halfway through, the total value is $1,000(1.0609) = $1,060.90. The interest paid by that point is $60.90. Therefore, the total interest over the entire period will be roughly double (and at least double), leaving only one viable answer.

The correct answer choice is (A).

If there are 6 more girls than boys in a room, and there are 14 boys and girls in the room, how many are girls?

- 4
- 5
- 8
- 10
- 12

A Difference and a Total

If there are 6 more girls than boys in a room, and there are 14 boys and girls in the room, how many are girls?

- ○ 4
- ○ 5
- ○ 8
- ○ 10
- ○ 12

Explanation

We can create variables B and G for the numbers of boys and girls. The first phrase tells us that $G = B + 6$. (We can pick numbers for a case to check that the 6 is on the correct side.) The second phrase tells us that $G + B = 14$. We want G. We can actually just add these two equations to obtain $2G + B = B + 20$. The B's drop and $G = 10$.

The correct answer is (D).

Working simultaneously at their respective constant rates, Machines A and B produce 20 widgets in c hours. Working alone at its constant rate, Machine A produces 20 widgets in a hours. In terms of a and c, how many hours does it take Machine B, working alone at its constant rate, to produce 10 widgets?

- $\dfrac{ac}{a+c}$
- $\dfrac{2ac}{a+c}$
- $\dfrac{ac}{2a+2c}$
- $\dfrac{ac}{2a-2c}$
- $\dfrac{ac}{2c-2a}$

A Machine's Rate of Production

Working simultaneously at their respective constant rates, Machines A and B produce 20 widgets in c hours. Working alone at its constant rate, Machine A produces 20 widgets in a hours. In terms of a and c, how many hours does it take Machine B, working alone at its constant rate, to produce 10 widgets?

- $\frac{ac}{a+c}$
- $\frac{2ac}{a+c}$
- $\frac{ac}{2a+2c}$
- $\frac{ac}{2a-2c}$
- $\frac{ac}{2c-2a}$

Explanation

The rates in this question can be expressed in terms of the units $\frac{widgets}{hours}$. The rate of the two machines working together is the sum of the independent rates. Therefore, we can write

$$\frac{20 \text{ widgets}}{a \text{ hours}} + \frac{10 \text{ widgets}}{b \text{ hours}} = \frac{20 \text{ widgets}}{c \text{ hours}}$$

The first term is Machine A's rate, the second is Machine B's rate, and the rate on the right side is their combined rate. We can get rid of the fractions by multiplying both sides of the equation by abc:

$$20bc + 10ac = 20ab$$

$$20bc - 20ab = -10ac$$

$$b(20c - 20a) = -10ac$$

$$b = \frac{-10ac}{20c - 20a}$$

$$b = \frac{-ac}{2c - 2a}$$

This doesn't appear in the answer choices, so we can reformat by multiplying by 1:

$$= \frac{-ac}{2c - 2a}\left(\frac{-1}{-1}\right) = \frac{ac}{2a - 2c}$$

For an alternate method, we can test with values. For example, looking at our first equation above, if $a=20$ and $b=10$, then both machines produce one widget together. Combined, they should produce twice as fast, so $c=10$. Plugging a and c into our solution, we can see whether we get b: $\frac{ac}{2a-2c} = \frac{(20)(10)}{2(20)-2(10)} = \frac{20}{4-2} = 10$. That worked as planned. Indeed, these values for c and a do not yield a proper value for b in any of the other equations. The correct answer is (D).

If k is an integer greater than 6, all of the following must be divisible by 3 EXCEPT

- $k(k+3)(k-1)$
- $3k^3$
- $(k+1)(k+5)(k+6)$
- $(k+2)(k-2)(k+3)$
- $k(k+1)(k+2)$

ALGEBRAIC DIVISIBILITY BY 3

If *k* is an integer greater than 6, all of the following must be divisible by 3 EXCEPT

- $k(k+3)(k-1)$
- $3k^3$
- $(k+1)(k+5)(k+6)$
- $(k+2)(k-2)(k+3)$
- $k(k+1)(k+2)$

EXPLANATION

In this question, we will eliminate any answer choice that we can demonstrate must be divisible by 3. And if we find an example in which any answer choice isn't divisible by three, that one is the correct answer. (B) has 3 as a factor, so it's divisible by 3 and is not the answer. There is a pattern in the other answer choices: they are variations on the theme that if you take any three consecutive integers, one of them will have to be divisible by three. In 3, 4, 5, it's 3; in 4, 5, 6, it's 6; in 5, 6, 7, it's 6. That way, if you multiply the three numbers, one will bring a factor of 3 into the final product. (A) seems to stand out because *k* and *k*+3 are redundant in this respect. We can try a number. Say *k*=5. Then $k(k+3)(k-1) = (5)(8)(4)$. That's not divisible by 3.

The correct answer is (A).

Machine A produces nails at a uniform rate of 120 every 10 seconds, and Machine B produces nails at a uniform rate of 100 every 15 seconds. If the two machines run simultaneously, how many seconds will it take for them to produce a total of 140 nails?

- 7.0
- 7.5
- 8.0
- 8.5
- 9.0

Combined Rate of Nail-Producing Machines

Machine A produces nails at a uniform rate of 120 every 10 seconds, and Machine B produces nails at a uniform rate of 100 every 15 seconds. If the two machines run simultaneously, how many seconds will it take for them to produce a total of 140 nails?

- 7.0
- 7.5
- 8.0
- 8.5
- 9.0

Explanation

Since these machines work independently, their rates add:

$$\frac{120 \text{ nails}}{10 \text{ seconds}} + \frac{100 \text{ nails}}{15 \text{ seconds}} = \frac{140 \text{ nails}}{x \text{ seconds}}$$

We almost have x. Simplifying and trying to avoid substantial computation:

$$\frac{12 \text{ nails}}{1 \text{ seconds}} + \frac{20 \text{ nails}}{3 \text{ seconds}} = \frac{140 \text{ nails}}{x \text{ seconds}}$$

$$\frac{36 \text{ nails}}{3 \text{ seconds}} + \frac{20 \text{ nails}}{3 \text{ seconds}} = \frac{140 \text{ nails}}{x \text{ seconds}}$$

$$\frac{56 \text{ nails}}{3 \text{ seconds}} = \frac{140 \text{ nails}}{x \text{ seconds}}$$

Cross-multiplying:

$$56x = (140)(3)$$

$$x = \frac{(140)(3)}{56} = \frac{(70)(2)(3)}{(28)(2)} = \frac{(35)(3)}{(14)} = \frac{105}{14}$$

And finally, we can perform the long division:

```
            7. 5
       ┌─────────
    14 │ 1 0 5. 0
           9 8
         ───────
             7 0
             7 0
         ───────
               0
```

The correct answer is (B).

A road declines 30° from horizontal over a distance of 60 feet, as measured by a tape on the road's surface. At the base of the incline is a hole 7 feet deep. What is the difference in elevation between the top of the incline and the bottom of the hole?

- 127
- 37
- 23
- $7 + 60\sqrt{3}$
- $7 + 30\sqrt{3}$

Decline in a Road

A road declines 30° from horizontal over a distance of 60 feet, as measured by a tape on the road's surface. At the base of the incline is a hole 7 feet deep. What is the difference in elevation between the top of the incline and the bottom of the hole?

- 127
- 37
- 23
- $7 + 60\sqrt{3}$
- $7 + 30\sqrt{3}$

Explanation

Most questions involving geometry warrant the brief effort to sketch a figure. For example, we want to be sure we capture "30 degrees from horizontal" correctly.

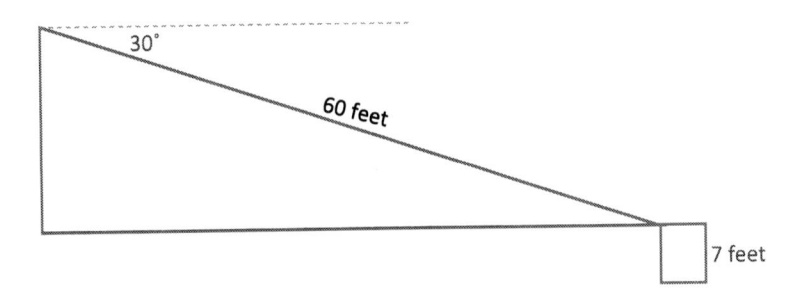

The triangle is a 30-60-90 triangle, because the top angle is 60 and it's a right triangle. We have the length of the side (60 feet) corresponding to the right angle, and we want to find the shortest side, the one measuring the vertical drop, which corresponds to the smallest angle, 30 degrees.

x	$2x$	$x\sqrt{3}$
30	60	

The drop is 30 feet. Adding the depth of the hole, the total drop is 37 feet.

The correct answer is (B).

If Ernesto were 15 years older, he would be 50% older than his wife. The sum of their ages is 90. What is Ernesto's current age?

- 48
- 50
- 52
- 54
- 56

Ernesto and His Wife's Ages

If Ernesto were 15 years older, he would be 50% older than his wife. The sum of their ages is 90. What is Ernesto's current age?

- 48
- 50
- 52
- 54
- 56

Explanation

If we call Ernesto's age E and his wife's age W, then we are told that $E + 15 = 1.5W$ and $E + W = 90$. We can substitute to solve. When you solve by substitution, you first isolate the variable you *don't* want at the end. So we isolate W: $W = 90 - E$ and then substitute:

$$E + 15 = 1.5(90 - E)$$

$$E + 15 = 135 - 1.5E$$

$$2.5E = 120$$

$$E = \frac{120}{2.5} = \frac{24}{0.5} = 48$$

This one is easy to check. The wife must be 42. If he were 15 years older, he'd be 63, which is 21 and hence 50% older than his wife.

The correct answer is (A).

Company X bought a shipment of light bulbs $3 per bulb, paid $1,200 to store and ship the bulbs, and later sold the bulbs for $13 per bulb. The gross profit earned from these sales is the total income from sales minus the total cost. If a batch contained 1,500 light bulbs, then Company X's gross profit per bulb is

- $8.80
- $9.00
- $9.20
- $9.80
- $10.00

Gross Profit per Light Bulb

Company X bought a shipment of light bulbs $3 per bulb, paid $1,200 to store and ship the bulbs, and later sold the bulbs for $13 per bulb. The gross profit earned from these sales is the total income from sales minus the total cost. If a batch contained 1,500 light bulbs, then Company X's gross profit per bulb is

- $8.80
- $9.00
- $9.20
- $9.80
- $10.00

Explanation

The question defines gross profit for us and then tells us it wants the gross profit *per bulb*, which will be the gross profit divided by the number of bulbs. Therefore, we are looking for

$$\text{gross profit per bulb} = \frac{\text{total income} - \text{total cost}}{\text{number of bulbs}}.$$

The income was $13 times the number of bulbs. There are two costs: $3 times the number of bulbs, and the flat cost of $1,200. And we have the number of bulbs: 1,500. Carefully plugging, we have

$$\text{gross profit per bulb} = \frac{13(1500) - (3(1500) + 1200)}{1500}$$

$$\text{gross profit per bulb} = \frac{13(1500) - 3(1500) - 1200}{1500}$$

$$\text{gross profit per bulb} = \frac{10(1500) - 1200}{1500} = 10 - \frac{4}{5} = 9.2$$

We could have jumped straight to this point: since the company is selling for $10 than it's buying, it's making $10 per bulb, minus the per-bulb price of the storage cost (which is $\frac{1200}{1500}$).

The correct answer is (C).

A store sold 50 sweaters, which usually are priced at x dollars, at 15 percent below the normal price. In terms of x, what was the total revenue from the sale of the sweaters?

- $\frac{85x}{2}$
- $\frac{3x}{2}$
- $42x$
- $50x - 15$
- $\frac{4.5}{x}$

Revenue from Sweaters

A store sold 50 sweaters, which usually are priced at x dollars, at 15 percent below the normal price. In terms of x, what was the total revenue from the sale of the sweaters?

- $\dfrac{85x}{2}$
- $\dfrac{3x}{2}$
- $42x$
- $50x - 15$
- $\dfrac{4.5}{x}$

Explanation

Since the normal price per sweater is x dollars, the lower price is $0.85x$. The total revenue is this price times the number of sweaters, so it's $(0.85x)(50)$. This is the same as $(85x)(.50)$, which is answer choice (A).

Note that we used a handy decimal-point trick: when you have an awkward multiplication with a decimal, you can freely move it to the other number, and sometimes it's easier. For example, if we have to take 80% of 3.75, we can reformat as $(0.8)(3.75)$ and pass the 0.1 to the second term, giving $(8)(0.375) = (8)\left(\dfrac{3}{8}\right) = 3$.

Again, the correct answer is (A).

In an increasing sequence of 8 consecutive odd integers, the sum of the first 4 integers is 656. What is the sum of the last 4 integers in the sequence?

- 688
- 692
- 696
- 700
- 704

Consecutive Odd Integers

In an increasing sequence of 8 consecutive odd integers, the sum of the first 4 integers is 656. What is the sum of the last 4 integers in the sequence?

- 688
- 692
- 696
- 700
- 704

Explanation

The missing word here is "average." For a life of simplified computations, when you hear the word "sum" you want to think "average" (and *vice versa*). We can use the cross-multiplied average formula:

$$\text{sum of items} = (\text{average of items})(\text{number of items}).$$

Let's apply it to the fact that the sum of the first 4 integers is 656:

$$656 = (\text{average of first 4 numbers})(4)$$

$$\text{average of first 4 numbers} = \frac{656}{4} = 164$$

If this is the average of consecutive odd integers, then the integers must be 161, 163, 165, and 167, which balance in pairs around 164. Therefore, the last four numbers in the sequence must be 169, 171, 173, 175. We could add these up to find the answer... or, we could use the average formula to find their sum! They are balanced around 172, so that is their average, and there are four of them, so

$$\text{sum of second 4 numbers} = (172)(4) = 400 + 280 + 8 = 688.$$

The correct answer is (A).

When positive integer *m* is divided by positive integer *n*, the remainder is 27. If $\frac{m}{n} = 75.018$, what is the value of *n*?

- 1800
- 1500
- 1280
- 750
- 480

Remainder and Fractional Portion

When positive integer *m* is divided by positive integer *n*, the remainder is 27. If $\frac{m}{n} = 75.018$, what is the value of *n*?

- 1800
- 1500
- 1280
- 750
- 480

Explanation

We are given two statements that convey similar information: both the remainder and the non-integer portion of the decimal describe the portion of the division that didn't happen cleanly. For example, if we divide 7 by 5, or $\frac{7}{5}$, the remainder is 2, and the decimal value of $\frac{7}{5}$ is $1\frac{2}{5} = 1.4$. And there's a relationship: it's the remainder of 2, over the divisor, 5, that gave us the decimal portion of .4. Therefore,

$$\frac{27}{n} = 0.018$$

$$n = \frac{27}{0.018} = \frac{9(3)}{9(0.002)} = \frac{3}{2 \times 10^{-3}} = \frac{3}{2} \times 10^3 = 1500.$$

The correct answer is (B).

If $y(3y-1) = 0$ and $\left(y + \frac{1}{3}\right)\left(y - \frac{1}{3}\right) = 0$, then $y =$

- -3
- $-\frac{1}{3}$
- 0
- $\frac{1}{3}$
- 3

Two Quadratic Equations

If $y(3y - 1) = 0$ and $\left(y + \frac{1}{3}\right)\left(y - \frac{1}{3}\right) = 0$, then $y =$

- ○ -3
- ○ $-\frac{1}{3}$
- ○ 0
- ○ $\frac{1}{3}$
- ○ 3

Explanation

Both of these equations given to us are factored quadratics set equal to zero. That's exactly what you want when solving a quadratic equation. When two things multiply to zero, one or the other must be zero, so you have narrowed it to two possibilities. The first equation tells us that either $y = 0$ or $3y - 1 = 0$, in which case $y = \frac{1}{3}$. The second equation tells us that either the first factor equals zero, in which case $y = -\frac{1}{3}$, or the second does, in which case $y = \frac{1}{3}$. We are told both statements are true, but there is only one case in which they can both be true, which is that $y = \frac{1}{3}$.

The correct answer is (D).

If the median of a series of C consecutive integers is M, and M is a member of the series, what is the smallest member of the series?

- $M - \frac{C-1}{2}$
- $M - \frac{C}{2}$
- $M - \frac{C}{2} - 1$
- $\frac{M-C-1}{2}$
- $\frac{M-C}{2}$

Algebraic Manipulation of a Median

If the median of a series of C consecutive integers is M, and M is a member of the series, what is the smallest member of the series?

- $M - \frac{C-1}{2}$
- $M - \frac{C}{2}$
- $M - \frac{C}{2} - 1$
- $\frac{M-C-1}{2}$
- $\frac{M-C}{2}$

Explanation

M is the median of a set of consecutive numbers and it's also a member, so we know the number of elements in this set is odd. Half the numbers are above and half below, except for the one in the middle. So (A) looks right. We can test with a case. Say our set is 7, 8, 9, 10, 11, which is a set of 5 integers, so *C*=5 and *M*=9. Indeed, we want to subtract $\frac{5-1}{2}$ from 9 to get 7. We can also see from this case that the other answer choices are incorrect.

The correct answer is (A).

$\frac{1}{3} + \left[\left(\frac{10}{7} \times \frac{7}{12}\right) \div 6\right] - \frac{11}{12} =$

- $\frac{13}{12}$
- $\frac{11}{12}$
- $\frac{1}{12}$
- 0
- $-\frac{4}{9}$

Arithmetic with Fractions

$$\frac{1}{3} + \left[\left(\frac{10}{7} \times \frac{7}{12}\right) \div 6\right] - \frac{11}{12} =$$

- $\frac{13}{12}$
- $\frac{11}{12}$
- $\frac{1}{12}$
- 0
- $-\frac{4}{9}$

Explanation

$$\frac{1}{3} + \left[\left(\frac{10}{7} \times \frac{7}{12}\right) \div 6\right] - \frac{11}{12}$$

$$\frac{1}{3} + \left[\left(\frac{10}{12}\right) \div 6\right] - \frac{11}{12}$$

$$\frac{1}{3} + \left[\left(\frac{10}{12}\right)\left(\frac{1}{6}\right)\right] - \frac{11}{12}$$

$$\frac{1}{3} + \left[\left(\frac{5}{6}\right)\left(\frac{1}{6}\right)\right] - \frac{11}{12}$$

$$\frac{1}{3} + \left[\left(\frac{5}{36}\right)\right] - \frac{11}{12}$$

$$\frac{12}{36} + \frac{5}{36} - \frac{33}{36}$$

$$\frac{12 + 5 - 33}{36}$$

$$\frac{17 - 33}{36}$$

$$\frac{-16}{36} = -\frac{4}{9}$$

The correct answer is (E).

The value of an investment decreased from $1,800 to $1,610. Approximately what was the percent decrease in value?

- 4%
- 11%
- 15%
- 25%
- 29%

PERCENT DECREASE IN VALUE

The value of an investment decreased from $1,800 to $1,610. Approximately what was the percent decrease in value?

- o 4%
- o 11%
- o 15%
- o 25%
- o 29%

EXPLANATION

In this question, we must determine a percentage change. Percentage changes are measured relative to the original value, which in this case is $1800. The change itself was $190. Therefore, the proportion of change, as a fraction, is $\frac{190}{1800}$. We have the word "approximately" in this question, so we can approximate. The fraction is roughly $\frac{2}{18}$, which is $\frac{1}{9}$, which is $0.\overline{11}$. The exact value might not be 11% exactly, but it will certainly be closer to 11% than to 15%.

The correct answer is (B).

On the Richter scale for measuring earthquake strength, an earthquake with a given reading on the scale is 10 times stronger than an earthquake with a reading of 1 less on the scale. If earthquake A measures 2 on the scale and earthquake B is 1,000 times stronger than earthquake A, how does earthquake B measure on the scale?

- 2^5
- 5
- 7.25
- $2(3^{10})$
- $2^{10} + 10^3$

Earthquake Strength

On the Richter scale for measuring earthquake strength, an earthquake with a given reading on the scale is 10 times stronger than an earthquake with a reading of 1 less on the scale. If earthquake A measures 2 on the scale and earthquake B is 1,000 times stronger than earthquake A, how does earthquake B measure on the scale?

- 2^5
- 5
- 7.25
- $2(3^{10})$
- $2^{10} + 10^3$

Explanation

The first sentence tells us that "ten times stronger" means "plus one on the scale." In the particular case at hand, therefore, we are talking about "1,000 times stronger," which is ten times stronger one time, so plus one on the scale; ten times stronger another time, so another plus one on the scale; and a final ten times stronger, so a third plus one on the scale, for a total of +3 on the scale. This is +3 relative to a reading of 2, so the reading of the stronger earthquake is 5.

The correct answer is (B).

In a water tank, $\frac{3}{4}$ of the volume is occupied by water and the remainder of the volume is occupied by air. If a contaminant occupies $\frac{1}{3}$ of the water, by volume, and 20 percent of the air, what percent of the volume of the water tank is contaminated?

- 25%
- 30%
- 32%
- 33%
- 34%

Contaminated Volume in a Tank

In a water tank, $\frac{3}{4}$ of the volume is occupied by water and the remainder of the volume is occupied by air. If a contaminant occupies $\frac{1}{3}$ of the water, by volume, and 20 percent of the air, what percent of the volume of the water tank is contaminated?

- 25%
- 30%
- 32%
- 33%
- 34%

Explanation

The volume of this contaminated tank is $\frac{3}{4}$ water and $\frac{1}{4}$ air. A third of the water volume, which is $\frac{3}{4}$ of the total, is contaminated, and a fifth of the air volume is contaminated, so the contaminated fraction is:

$$\frac{3}{4}\left(\frac{1}{3}\right) + \frac{1}{4}\left(\frac{1}{5}\right)$$

$$\frac{1}{4} + \frac{1}{20} = \frac{5}{20} + \frac{1}{20} = \frac{6}{20} \times \frac{5}{5} = \frac{30}{100}$$

If the setup isn't clear, you can clarify it (or avoid it) by considering the case in which the total volume is 60 (60 is often useful as an example when you have to do lots of dividing, because it's divisible by so many small numbers). Then 45 of the volume is water, and 15 of that 45 is contaminated; similarly, you'll find a volume of 3 for the air is polluted, for a total of $\frac{18}{60}$, which is $\frac{6}{20}$ and hence gives the same result.

The correct answer is (B).

A random sample of citizens contains people registered to vote and not registered to vote in the ratio 12:5, respectively. How many people not registered to vote are there if the sample contains 153 people?

- 9
- 33
- 37
- 45
- 47

People Registered to Vote

A random sample of citizens contains people registered to vote and not registered to vote in the ratio 12:5, respectively. How many people not registered to vote are there if the sample contains 153 people?

- 9
- 33
- 37
- 45
- 47

Explanation

If we call the number of people registered R and those "not" N, then we have

$$\frac{R}{N} = \frac{12}{5}$$

And

$$R + N = 153$$

We want N, so we can isolate R as $R = \frac{12}{5}N$ and substitute:

$$\frac{12}{5}N + N = 153$$

$$12N + 5N = 5(153)$$

$$17N = 5(153)$$

$$N = \frac{5(153)}{17}$$

$$N = \frac{5(3)(51)}{17}$$

$$N = 5(3)(3) = 45$$

The correct answer is (D).

The present ratio of apples to oranges within a basket is 10 to 1. If 18 apples and 3 oranges were added, the ratio of apples to oranges would be 7 to 1. How many apples are in the basket?

- 10
- 16
- 20
- 24
- 30

Changing an Apples-to-Oranges Ratio

The present ratio of apples to oranges within a basket is 10 to 1. If 18 apples and 3 oranges were added, the ratio of apples to oranges would be 7 to 1. How many apples are in the basket?

- 10
- 16
- 20
- 24
- 30

Explanation

In this question, the numbers in both the question and the answer choices are pretty friendly, so it's a good candidate for the old "plug in the answer choices and see which one works" method. For example, we can try (B). Actually, that would give us a fractional number of oranges, which won't work. So (B) and (D) are out. Let's try (C):

$$A = 20; R = 2$$

$$A + 18 = 38; R + 3 = 5$$

The ratio is close to 7 to 1, but it's a bit too wide.

$$A = 10; R = 1$$

$$A + 18 = 28; R + 3 = 4$$

This gives the correct 7-to-1 ratio.

The correct answer is (A).

One scanning device, working at a constant rate, can scan the pages of a particular book in 11 minutes. A second scanning device, working at a constant rate, can scan the same book in 5 minutes. If both scanning devices are used on different copies of the book, one working from the front and one from the back, approximately how many minutes are required to scan the pages of the book?

- 0.89
- 1.44
- 2.80
- 3.44
- 4.33

Scanning the Pages of a Book

One scanning device, working at a constant rate, can scan the pages of a particular book in 11 minutes. A second scanning device, working at a constant rate, can scan the same book in 5 minutes. If both scanning devices are used on different copies of the book, one working from the front and one from the back, approximately how many minutes are required to scan the pages of the book?

- 0.89
- 1.44
- 2.80
- 3.44
- 4.33

Explanation

The rates here are measured in either pages per minute or books per minute. We can use pages and call P the number of pages in this book. The combined rate of using both scanners will be the sum of their individual rates:

$$\frac{P \text{ pages}}{11 \text{ min}} + \frac{P \text{ pages}}{5 \text{ min}} = \frac{P \text{ pages}}{x \text{ min}}$$

The variable P cancels out and we can multiply both sides by $55x$:

$$5x + 11x = 55$$

$$16x = 55$$

$$x = \frac{55}{16}$$

Since $16(3) = 48$, this fraction equals "three point something."

The correct answer is (D).

What is the approximate length, in inches, of the diagonal of a square of an area of 200 square inches?

- 15
- 20
- 25
- 27
- 29

The Diagonal of a Square

What is the approximate length, in inches, of the diagonal of a square of an area of 200 square inches?

- 15
- 20
- 25
- 27
- 29

Explanation

The diagonal of a square is the hypotenuse of a 45-45-90 triangle whose two equal sides are sides of the square. Meanwhile, the area of this square is $s^2 = 200$, so a side of the square is $\sqrt{200}$. Hence, the equal sides of the triangle in question are each $\sqrt{200}$. The sides of a 45-45-90 are in the ratio $x:x:x\sqrt{2}$, so in this case we can say $x = \sqrt{200}$ and therefore $x\sqrt{2} = \sqrt{2}\sqrt{200}$. Finally, $\sqrt{2}\sqrt{200} = \sqrt{400} = 20$.

The correct answer is (B).

Each year for 4 years, an insect species increased its population within a locality by the number equal to half of the population of the preceding year. If there were 16,200 insects of the species in the locality at the end of the four-year period, how many insects of the species were in the locality at the beginning of the four-year period?

- 2,600
- 2,800
- 3,000
- 3,200
- 3,400

Insect Population Growth

Each year for 4 years, an insect species increased its population within a locality by the number equal to half of the population of the preceding year. If there were 16,200 insects of the species in the locality at the end of the four-year period, how many insects of the species were in the locality at the beginning of the four-year period?

- 2,600
- 2,800
- 3,000
- 3,200
- 3,400

Explanation

The question is telling us that, if the population in a given year was 100, then in the next year it increased by $\frac{100}{2}$ = 50 to 150. Or, if it was x in a given year, it increased by $\frac{x}{2}$ to $\frac{3}{2}x$ in the following year. One way of working this problem would be to make a table of the insect count per year, and work it either backward from 16,200, or forward from a variable. Another way to approach this question is to think of it as a compound interest formula. (It's compound because the new insects beget more insects each year.) The formula is a bit faster. We are measuring between the beginning and the end of a 4-year period, so we have 4 full years of growth. Therefore, if we think of our initial population – or "principal," in investment terms – as P, the total growth is captured by:

$$16,200 = P(1.5)^4$$

$$16,200 = P\left(\frac{3}{2}\right)^4$$

$$16,200 = P\frac{81}{16}$$

$$P = \frac{16}{81} 16,200$$

The digits 1 + 6 + 2 + 0 + 0 = 9, so 16,200 is divisible by 9.

$$P = \frac{16}{81}(9 \times 1800)$$

$$P = \frac{16}{81}(9 \times 9 \times 200)$$

$$P = 16 \times 200 = 3200.$$

The correct answer is (D).

For the positive numbers, $k, k+1, k-2, k+3$, what is the ratio of the mean to the median?

- 1
- 2
- $\dfrac{k+1}{2}$
- $\dfrac{2k+1}{k}$
- $\dfrac{2k+2}{2k-1}$

Ratio of Mean to Median

For the positive numbers, $k, k+1, k-2, k+3$, what is the ratio of the mean to the median?

- 1
- 2
- $\frac{k+1}{2}$
- $\frac{2k+1}{k}$
- $\frac{2k+2}{2k-1}$

Explanation

In this question to find the mean of these four numbers, we add them up and divide by four:

$$\text{mean} = \frac{k + k + 1 + k - 2 + k + 3}{4}$$

$$= \frac{4k + 2}{4}$$

$$= k + \frac{1}{2}$$

To find the median, we must order the list: $\{k - 2, k, k + 1, k + 3\}$. Since there are an even number of elements in this list, the median is the average of the middle two:

$$\text{median} = \frac{2k + 1}{2}$$

$$= k + \frac{1}{2}$$

The mean and the median are the same, so their ratio is 1.

The correct answer is (A).

Sixty-four percent of the members of a study group are aged 30 or older, and 12.5 percent of those individuals aged 30 or older are teachers. If one member of the study group is to be selected at random, what is the probability that the member selected is a teacher aged 30 or older?

- 0.080
- 0.100
- 0.125
- 0.150
- 0.165

Teachers Aged 30+

Sixty-four percent of the members of a study group are aged 30 or older, and 12.5 percent of those individuals aged 30 or older are teachers. If one member of the study group is to be selected at random, what is the probability that the member selected is a teacher aged 30 or older?

- 0.080
- 0.100
- 0.125
- 0.150
- 0.165

Explanation

This question hasn't told us how many people are in the study group, and evidently therefore the answer doesn't depend on this value, so let's imagine 100 people are in the study group. Then, 64% or 64 people are aged 30 or older. Of that 64, 12.5% are teachers. 12.5% is $\frac{1}{8}$ (it's half a quarter), so as $\frac{1}{8}$ of 64 it represents 8 people. The odds of choosing one of these 8 people randomly from the group are $\frac{8}{100}$, since there are 100 people. So the probability is 8%.

The correct answer is (A).

If $N = \frac{5}{7}(M - 12)$, and if $N = 280$, then $M =$

- $\frac{1{,}340}{7}$
- 302
- 380
- 404
- $\frac{1{,}876}{5}$

Linear Equations with Fractions

If $N = \frac{5}{7}(M - 12)$, and if $N = 280$, then $M =$

- $\frac{1,340}{7}$
- 302
- 380
- 404
- $\frac{1,876}{5}$

Explanation

We can plug the value of N into the given equation:

$$280 = \frac{5}{7}(M - 12)$$

$$\frac{7}{5}(280) = \left(\frac{5}{7}(M - 12)\right)\frac{7}{5}$$

$$\frac{7}{5}(280) = M - 12$$

$$7(56) = M - 12$$

$$M = 7(56) + 12$$

$$M = 350 + 42 + 12 = 404$$

The correct answer is (D).

If 2^n is a divisor of 1680 and 2^m is not a divisor of 1680, where $m = n + 1$, what is the value of n?

- 2
- 3
- 4
- 5
- 6

Maximum Divisors

If 2^n is a divisor of 1680 and 2^m is not a divisor of 1680, where $m = n + 1$, what is the value of n?

- 2
- 3
- 4
- 5
- 6

Explanation

We are talking about divisors of 1680, which are numbers that go evenly into 1680. If we make a fraction with 1680 in the numerator and a divisor in the denominator, the fraction yields an integer. For this to happen, all of the factors that are present in the divisor must be 1680. Therefore, 1680 includes n 2's, since 2^n is a divisor, but 1680 does not have m 2's, since 2^m is not a divisor. Evidently, m is one 2 too many. So let's see how many 2's are in 1680, through repeated division.

$$
\begin{array}{cc}
& 1680 \\
2 & 840 \\
2 & 420 \\
2 & 210 \\
2 & 105 \\
5 & 21 \\
3 & 7 \\
\end{array}
$$

Therefore, the prime factorization is $1680 = 2^4 \times 3 \times 5 \times 7$. Therefore, $n = 4$ and $m = 5$.

The correct answer is (C)

What is the largest integer k for which $81^k < 3^{27}$?

- 6
- 7
- 8
- 9
- 10

Comparing Exponents

What is the largest integer k for which $81^k < 3^{27}$?

- 6
- 7
- 8
- 9
- 10

Explanation

When we prefer to compare or otherwise work with exponents of different bases, as in this question, we should first check to see whether we can convert them into the same base. We are asked whether the following is true:

$$81^k < 3^{27}$$

$$(9 \times 9)^k < 3^{27}$$

$$(3^2 \times 3^2)^k < 3^{27}$$

$$(3^4)^k < 3^{27}$$

$$3^{4k} < 3^{27}$$

We can consider some values of k. If $k = 6$, then $3^{4k} = 3^{24}$. That's less than 3^{27}, which is 3^{24} multiplied by three more 3's. If $k = 7$, then $3^{4k} = 3^{28}$. That's larger than 3^{27}, as it 3^{27} times one more 3, since 3^{28} is in fact three times larger than 3^{27}. Therefore, $k = 6$ is the last value before the left side gets bigger than the right side.

The correct answer is (A).

For the positive integers a and b, $k'(a,b)$ represents the number of zeros between the decimal point and the first nonzero digit to the right of the decimal point in the reciprocal of the product of a and b, when that reciprocal is expressed as a terminating decimal. What is the value of $k'(6^5, 5^6)$?

- 7
- 8
- 9
- 10
- 11

Counting Zeroes

For the positive integers *a* and *b*, $k'(a,b)$ represents the number of zeros between the decimal point and the first nonzero digit to the right of the decimal point in the reciprocal of the product of *a* and *b*, when that reciprocal is expressed as a terminating decimal. What is the value of $k'(6^5, 5^6)$?

- 7
- 8
- 9
- 10
- 11

Explanation

We're given the definition of a function and we are asked to evaluate the function for the pair of numbers 6^5 and 5^6. The reciprocal of the product of these numbers is

$$\frac{1}{6^5 5^6}.$$

We need to get this thing into a decimal notation. One approach would be to compute $6^5 5^6$ and perform long division with the result. Another would be compute 6^5 and 5^6, separately, compute $\frac{1}{6^5}$ and $\frac{1}{5^6}$ by long division, and multiply the two results. Both of these approaches would be time-prohibitive, so there must be a simpler way. The number $6^5 5^6$ could be reformatted as $(6 \times 5)^5 \times 5$, or $(30)^5 \times 5$, which is more computable. But the 30 there gives me the idea to separate out powers of 10:

$$= \frac{1}{2^5 3^5 5^6}$$

$$= \frac{1}{(2^5 5^5) 3^5 5} = \frac{1}{(2 \times 5)^5 3^5 5} = \frac{1}{(10)^5 3^5 5}$$

$$= \frac{1}{3^5 5} \times \frac{1}{10^5}$$

Now we must calculate. $3^5 5 = 243 \times 5 = 1{,}000 + 200 + 15 = 1215$. Beginning the $\frac{1}{1215}$ computation by long division, we get

```
        0. 0  0  0  8
1215 | 1. 0  0  0  0  0  0
```

We can stop here, since we are counting zeroes, not going for an actual value. The number $\frac{1}{1215}$ in decimal form has 3 zeroes to the right of the decimal point before the first significant digit. Multiplying by $\frac{1}{10^5}$ will add 5 zeroes, so the total number of zeroes is 8. The correct answer is (B).

Last year, Company X spent $3 million to manufacture consumer goods that obtained $50 million in sales revenue. This year, Company X spent $5 million to manufacture goods that obtained $98 in sales revenue. By approximately what percent did the ratio of manufacturing costs to sales revenue decrease from last year to this year?

- 6%
- 8%
- 15%
- 25%
- 30%

Change in Sales Ratio

Last year, Company X spent $3 million to manufacture consumer goods that obtained $50 million in sales revenue. This year, Company X spent $5 million to manufacture goods that obtained $98 in sales revenue. By approximately what percent did the ratio of manufacturing costs to sales revenue decrease from last year to this year?

- 6%
- 8%
- 15%
- 25%
- 30%

Explanation

Let's write the ratio as a fraction with units. We want to know the percent decrease of this thing:

$$\frac{\text{manufacturing costs}}{\text{sales revenue}}$$

Last year, it was $\frac{3}{50}$. This year, it was $\frac{5}{98}$. Since $\frac{3}{50} = \frac{6}{100}$ and $\frac{5}{98} \approx \frac{5}{100}$, the ratio has decreased from 0.06 to about 0.05. The percent change is the difference over the original value, so it's approximately $\frac{0.01}{0.06} \times 100\%$, or 17%. This is much closer to 15% than 25%.

The correct answer is (C).

If *n* is the product of the even integers from 10 to 20, inclusive, what is the second-greatest integer *m* for which 2^m is a factor of *n*?

- 9
- 10
- 11
- 12
- 18

Factor of a Large Product

If n is the product of the even integers from 10 to 20, inclusive, what is the second-greatest integer m for which 2^m is a factor of n?

- 9
- 10
- 11
- 12
- 18

Explanation

We can write out exactly what n is with no trouble. It's

$$n = 10 \times 12 \times 14 \times 16 \times 18 \times 20$$

Converting this into prime factors:

$$n = (2)(5) \times (2^2)(3) \times (2)(7) \times (2^4) \times (2)(3^2) \times (2^2)(5) = 2^{11}3^3 5^2 7$$

That means that 2^{11} is the greatest power of 2 that is a factor of n. The second-greatest is 2^{10}.

The correct answer is (B).

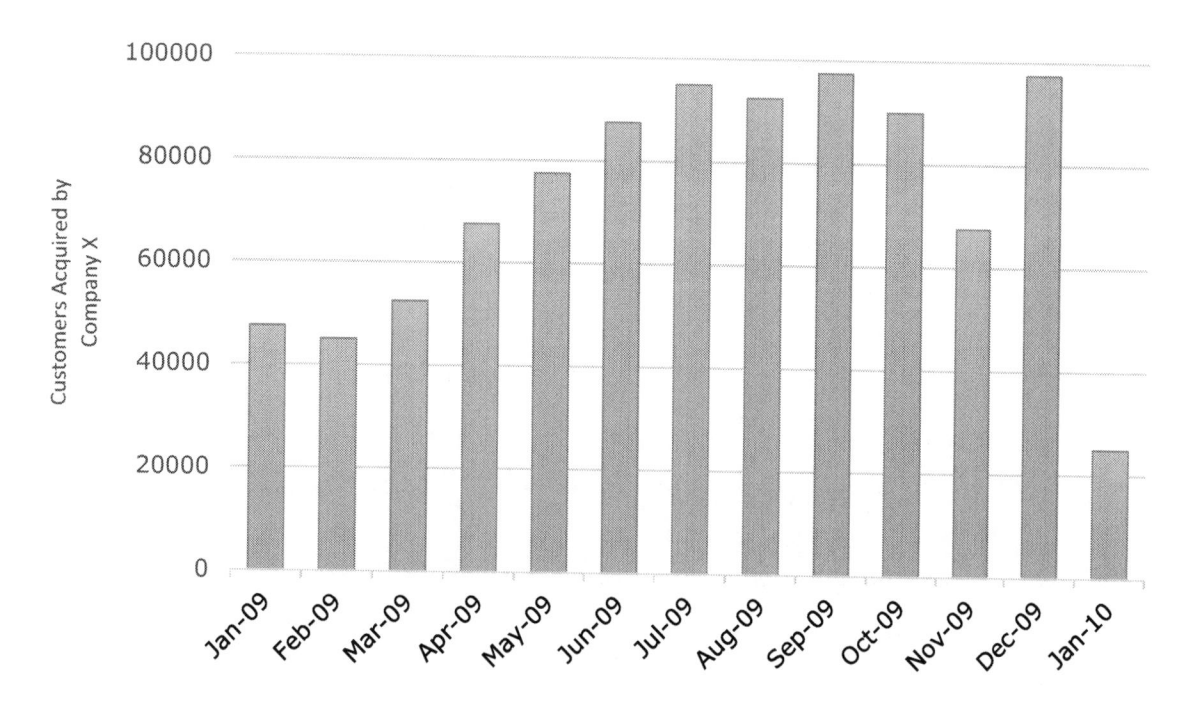

In the chart shown, which of the following is closest to the median monthly number of customers acquired by Company X?

- 62,500
- 70,000
- 77,500
- 81,250
- 85,000

Monthly Customer Acquisition

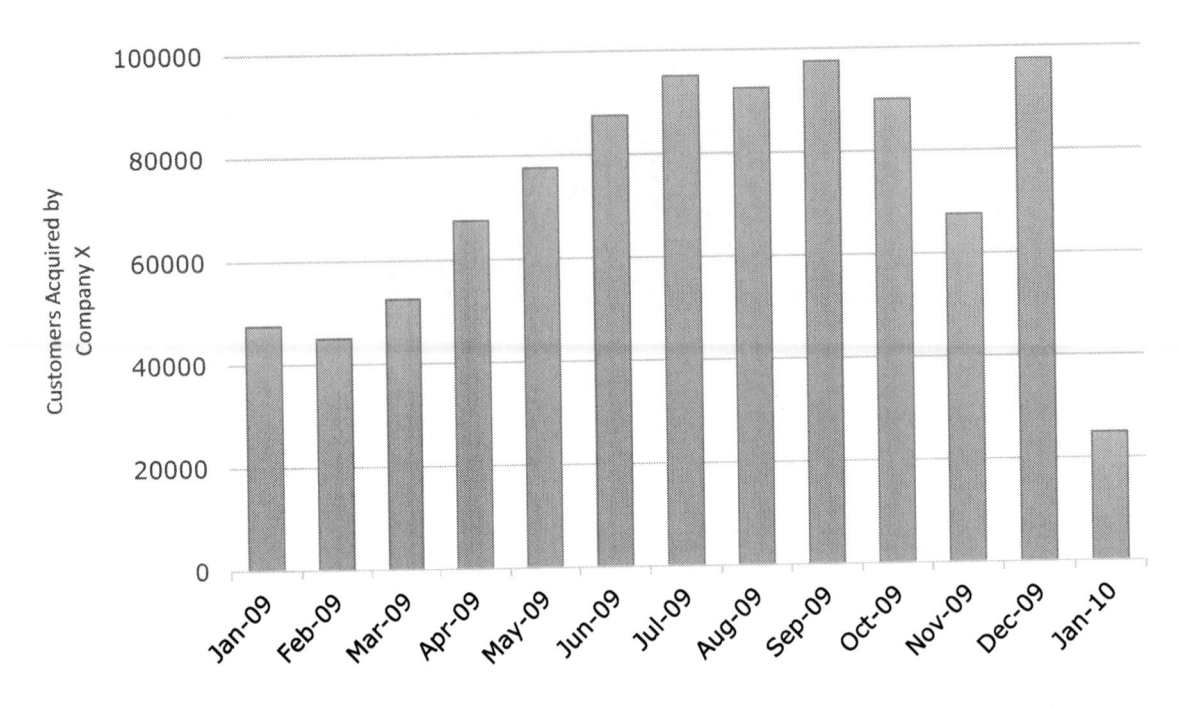

In the chart shown, which of the following is closest to the median monthly number of customers acquired by Company X?

- 62,500
- 70,000
- 77,500
- 81,250
- 85,000

Explanation

We must answer this question by eyeball, counting the number of vertical bars, determining the bar of middle height in this set, and estimating its height. There are 13 bars. To find the middle, we can count from the smallest or the tallest. Let's do smallest. The right bar is shortest; that's 1. The three leftmost bars are next shortest; those are 2, 3 and 4. Next to them and third from right are two bars of similar height; those are 5 and 6. So number 7 is the fifth bar in from the left. It is under 80,000, but easily more than half the distance from 60,000 to 80,000.

The correct answer is (C).

A certain characteristic in a large population has a distribution that is symmetric about the mean m. If 95 percent of the distribution lies within twice the standard deviation of the mean, where the standard deviation is d, what percent of the distribution is greater than $m + 2d$?

- 1%
- 2.5%
- 5%
- 95%
- 100%

GFPS114

SYMMETRIC DISTRIBUTION

A certain characteristic in a large population has a distribution that is symmetric about the mean m. If 95 percent of the distribution lies within twice the standard deviation of the mean, where the standard deviation is d, what percent of the distribution is greater than $m + 2d$?

- 1%
- 2.5%
- 5%
- 95%
- 100%

EXPLANATION

This question describes something that sounds like a normal distribution, although there is no mention of normal distributions in the official test rubric and so we won't have to bust out special statistics knowledge here. The distribution *might* look something like this:

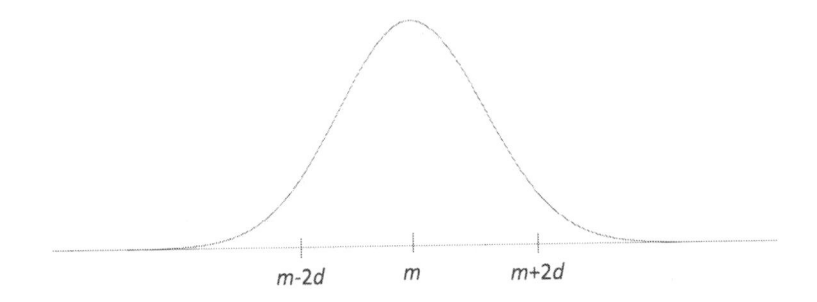

It's symmetric about the mean m. We're told 95 percent of the distribution lies between $m - 2d$ and $m + 2d$. That means that 5 percent of the distribution lies in the little portion to the left of $m - 2d$ and the little portion to the right of $m + 2d$. Since the distribution is symmetric, regardless of its exact shape, we know those two little portions are equal in size. Therefore the size of one of them must be half of 5 percent, or 2.5%.

The correct answer is (B).

A major company's satisfaction rate, defined as the percentage of its employees who identified themselves as "extremely satisfied" or "generally satisfied" with their jobs in a survey, dropped from 76 percent on January 1, 2005, to 68 percent on January 1, 2008. If the number of employees was 25 percent less on January 1, 2008, than on January 1, 2005, what was the approximate percent change in the number of satisfied employees at the company over this period?

- 50% decrease
- 33% decrease
- 15% increase
- 33% increase
- 55% increase

Company Satisfaction Rate

A major company's satisfaction rate, defined as the percentage of its employees who identified themselves as "extremely satisfied" or "generally satisfied" with their jobs in a survey, dropped from 76 percent on January 1, 2005, to 68 percent on January 1, 2008. If the number of employees was 25 percent less on January 1, 2008, than on January 1, 2005, what was the approximate percent change in the number of satisfied employees at the company over this period?

- 50% decrease
- 33% decrease
- 15% increase
- 33% increase
- 55% increase

Explanation

In this question, let's suppose that the company had 100 people in 2005. That means that 76 people were satisfied. In 2008, there were 75 total people, and 68% of them were satisfied. So the number of satisfied people in 2008 is 75(0.68). The percent change in the number of satisfied people will be the difference over the original, or:

$$\frac{75(0.68) - 76}{76}$$

We are allowed to approximate, so we can say

$$\approx \frac{76(0.68) - 76}{76}$$

$$= 0.68 - 1 = -0.32$$

Hence, our estimate is a 32% decrease in the number of satisfied people.

The correct answer is (B).

If $p = 5^6 - 2^6$, which of the following is NOT a factor of p?

- 91
- 19
- 13
- 5
- 3

Finding a Non-Factor

If $p = 5^6 - 2^6$, which of the following is NOT a factor of p?

- 91
- 19
- 13
- 5
- 3

Explanation

We could feasibly compute p directly, but it would be ugly, and we'd need to break it down into factors afterwards. As given, p is a difference of perfect squares, and we should always be on the lookout for those.

$$5^6 - 2^6 = (5^3 + 2^3)(5^3 - 2^3)$$

$$(125 + 8)(125 - 8)$$

$$(133)(117)$$

$$(7)(19)(3)(39)$$

$$(7)(19)(3)(3)(13)$$

The number 5 is not part of this set. The correct answer is (D).

Within a legislative body, the ratio of the number of women to the number of men was $\frac{3}{5}$. After 20 women and 10 men were added to the body, the ratio of the number of women to the number of men was $\frac{7}{10}$. After these additions, how many more members of the legislative body were men than women?

- 14
- 42
- 96
- 136
- 144

GFPS117

Ratio of Women to Men

Within a legislative body, the ratio of the number of women to the number of men was $\frac{3}{5}$. After 20 women and 10 men were added to the body, the ratio of the number of women to the number of men was $\frac{7}{10}$. After these additions, how many more members of the legislative body were men than women?

- 14
- 42
- 96
- 136
- 144

Explanation

In this question, the answer choices are friendly, round, numbers, so we can guess an answer choice and work it backwards to see whether it's correct.

We are looking for the difference in men and women after the addition, when the ratio is $\frac{7}{10}$. This difference can be expressed as $10n - 7n = 3n$, where n is an integer. So the correct answer will be divisible by 3. That means that choice (D) is definitely out, because the digits in (D) don't sum to a number that is divisible by 3.

We can try choice (C). If (C) is correct, then the final difference is $3n = 96$, $n = 32$, and the final numbers of men and women are $10n = 320$ men and $7n = 32(7) = 210 + 14 = 234$ women. In that case, prior to the additions, this means 214 women and 310 men. These are supposed to be in a ratio of 3 to 5, but $2 + 1 + 4 = 7$ isn't even divisible by 3. That means that answer choice (C) cannot be correct.

We can try (B). If (B) is correct, then the final difference is $3n = 42$ and $n = 14$. The men are $10n = 140$ and the women are $7n = 14(7) = 98$ in the final ratio. In this case, prior to additions, the men are 130 and the women are 78. Is 78 to 130 a ratio of 3 to 5? We try $\frac{78}{3} \times 5 = 26 \times 5 = 130$. Working backward was successful in this case, so we have our correct answer.

Note that, if (B) hadn't been correct, we would be left with only (A) and (E) as possibilities, and we likely would have been able to choose one over the other by identifying whether we needed larger or smaller numbers than in choice (B).

The correct answer is (B).

The organizers of a conference offered a certain number of simultaneous seminars with the intention that each seminar would be attended by 18 conference attendees. However, space limitations allowed only up to 15 conference attendees to participate in each of a number of the seminars, leaving 4 remaining seminars that together would be attended by at least 93 conference attendees. How many seminars were there?

- 10
- 11
- 15
- 20
- 26

Seminar Overflow

The organizers of a conference offered a certain number of simultaneous seminars with the intention that each seminar would be attended by 18 conference attendees. However, space limitations allowed only up to 15 conference attendees to participate in each of a number of the seminars, leaving 4 remaining seminars that together would be attended by at least 93 conference attendees. How many seminars were there?

- 10
- 11
- 15
- 20
- 26

Explanation

This question is prone to algebra errors and it has friendly answer choices, so I'll prefer to analyze it by cases, using the answer choices. I'll start with (A), 10, since it's easy to work with, and then I can double it to get a sense of (D) and the answer choices in between. If the answer is 10, 10 is the number of seminars. In that case, there are 4 unconstrained seminars, originally designed for 18 attendees each, and 6 constrained seminars, originally designed for 18 attendees each but constrained to 15 attendees each. The minimum number of attendees that would attend the four unconstrained one is, first, 4×18 (since the other ones are overful anyway, they have no where else to go) *plus* the overflow, which in this case must be $18 - 15 = 3$ people per constrained seminar, of which there are 6, giving us

$$(4 \times 18) + (6 \times 3)$$

$$= (4 \times 18) + 18$$

$$= 5 \times 18 = 50 + 40 = 90$$

That's supposed to be the minimum number of attendees in the 4 unconstrained sessions, but it's too small, because we are told that number is 93. However, I can see that adding one constrained seminar will increase the overflow by 3, making this sum correct.

The correct answer is (B).

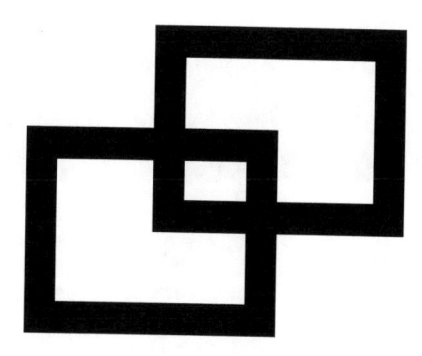

A wooden frame 1 foot wide has been constructed around each of two rectangular sheets of glass measuring 4 feet by 5 feet. If the area of overlapping glass in the figure above measures 1 foot by 2 feet, what fraction of the total area of the glass sheets and wooden frames is overlapping?

- $\dfrac{1}{21}$
- $\dfrac{1}{10}$
- $\dfrac{6}{21}$
- $\dfrac{1}{2}$
- $\dfrac{5}{8}$

Overlapping Frames

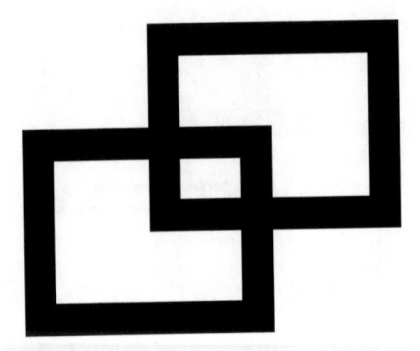

A wooden frame 1 foot wide has been constructed around each of two rectangular sheets of glass measuring 4 feet by 5 feet. If the area of overlapping glass in the figure above measures 1 foot by 2 feet, what fraction of the total area of the glass sheets and wooden frames is overlapping?

- $\frac{1}{21}$
- $\frac{1}{10}$
- $\frac{6}{21}$
- $\frac{1}{2}$
- $\frac{5}{8}$

Explanation

In this question, the overlapping area of glass plus frame is the white rectangle in the middle with the black border around that white rectangle. However, some portion of the frame is overlapping, making that part confusing. Let's just consider the overlapping portion of the lower left window-plus-frame. Let's ignore the distinction between frame and non-frame and focus on total area. In that case, the entire lower left window-plus-frame is a rectangle measuring $(4 + 1 + 1) \times (5 + 1 + 1) = 6 \times 7 = 42$. We have to add the two along each dimenion, since it's on both sides in each dimension. And the smaller rectangle, the portion of overlap, measures $(1 + 1 + 1) \times (2 + 1 + 1) = 3 \times 4 = 12$. The fraction of one rectangle that overlaps is $\frac{12}{42}$, and this stays the same when we add an identical rectangle of equal overlap. Therefore the correct answer is $\frac{12}{42} = \frac{6}{21}$.

The correct answer is (C).

If $a = -0.5$, then each of the following must be true EXCEPT

- $a < a^2$
- $a^3 < a^2$
- $a < a^3$
- $a^2 < a^4$
- $a^3 < a^5$

INEQUALITIES WITH A NEGATIVE FRACTION

If $a = -0.5$, then each of the following must be true EXCEPT

- $a < a^2$
- $a^3 < a^2$
- $a < a^3$
- $a^2 < a^4$
- $a^3 < a^5$

EXPLANATION

In this question, a has two key attributes: first, that it is negative, and second, that is a fraction of absolute value less than one. The first fact means that it will be positive at even powers and negative at odd powers, like any negative number. The fractional nature means that its absolute value gets smaller as it's taken to higher powers, although, since it's also negative, it still flops back and forth between positive and negative. Digging in, (A) is true, because $-\frac{1}{2} < \frac{1}{4}$; the first is left of the other on the number line. Choice (B) is correct, because $-\frac{1}{8} < \frac{1}{4}$. Choice (C) is correct, because $-\frac{1}{2}$ is left of $-\frac{1}{8}$ on the number line. Choice (E) correct in a similar way to (C). Choice (D) says that $\frac{1}{4} < \frac{1}{16}$, which is false.

The correct answer is (D).

The ratio of the height of a regular cylindrical container to the radius of its base is approximately 4.3 to 3. If the radius of the base is 6 meters, what is the approximate height of the container, in meters?

- 5
- 7
- 9
- 13
- 26

Ratio of a Cylinder's Dimensions

The ratio of the height of a regular cylindrical container to the radius of its base is approximately 4.3 to 3. If the radius of the base is 6 meters, what is the approximate height of the container, in meters?

- 5
- 7
- 9
- 13
- 26

Explanation

We have a ratio with two parts, so we can write it as a fraction with units:

$$\frac{4.3 \text{ m high}}{3 \text{ m radius}}$$

This ratio is constant throughout this question, so we can set one instance of the ratio equal to another:

$$\frac{4.3 \text{ m high}}{3 \text{ m radius}} = \frac{x \text{ m high}}{6 \text{ m radius}}$$

We could cross-multiply and solve to find x, but we can also see that the denominator on the right is twice that of the left, so the numerator on the right must be twice that of the left, hence $4.3 \times 2 = 8.6$. The closest approximate choice is 9.

The correct answer is (C).

If $3 < y < 150$, for how many values of y is the square root of y twice a prime number?

- Two
- Three
- Four
- Five
- Six

Prime Number Manipulation

If $3 < y < 150$, for how many values of y is the square root of y twice a prime number?

- Two
- Three
- Four
- Five
- Six

Explanation

This question describes what might sound like a lot of numbers, but as we can see from the answer choices, we're talking about a maximum of six. So we should be able to enumerate the cases exactly. We are talking about a number whose square root is twice a prime number. Let's work that backwards, starting with a prime number. How about 5. Twice this prime number is 10, and if 10 is the square root of y, then $y=100$. More systematically, we can make a list of primes and the corresponding values of y:

prime	double	squared=y
2	4	16
3	6	36
5	10	100
7	14	196

The last case is already too big, since $196 > 150$. And all other possibilities will be only larger, so the correct answer is 3.

The correct answer is (B).

If $a > 0$ and $\frac{a}{b} = \sqrt{b}$, what is b in terms of a?

- $\frac{1}{a}$
- $\sqrt{a}$
- $a\sqrt{a}$
- $a^{\frac{2}{3}}$
- $a^3 - a^2$

Solving by Exponent Rules

If $a > 0$ and $\frac{a}{b} = \sqrt{b}$, what is b in terms of a?

- $\frac{1}{a}$
- $\sqrt{a}$
- $a\sqrt{a}$
- $a^{\frac{2}{3}}$
- $a^3 - a^2$

Explanation

We can do a little algebraic work here but be prepared to analyze by cases. We want to know about b, so we want to isolate b:

$$\frac{a}{b} = \sqrt{b}$$

$$a = b\sqrt{b}$$

The right side is b to the first power times b to the $\frac{1}{2}$ power, so it's

$$a = b^{\frac{3}{2}}$$

$$(a)^{\frac{2}{3}} = \left(b^{\frac{3}{2}}\right)^{\frac{2}{3}}$$

$$b = a^{\frac{2}{3}}$$

The correct answer is (D).

$$n, m, p, q, r$$

An arithmetic sequence is a sequence in which each term after the first is equal to the sum of the preceding term and a constant. If the list of letters shown above is an arithmetic sequence, which of the following must also be an arithmetic sequence?

I. $3n, 3m, 3p, 3q, 3r$

II. $n-2, m-2, p-2, q-2, r-2$

III. n^3, m^3, p^3, q^3, r^3

- I only
- II only
- III only
- I and II
- II and III

Arithmetic Sequence

$$n, m, p, q, r$$

An arithmetic sequence is a sequence in which each term after the first is equal to the sum of the preceding term and a constant. If the list of letters shown above is an arithmetic sequence, which of the following must also be an arithmetic sequence?

I. $3n, 3m, 3p, 3q, 3r$

II. $n-2, m-2, p-2, q-2, r-2$

III. n^3, m^3, p^3, q^3, r^3

- I only
- II only
- III only
- I and II
- II and III

Explanation

In this question, we can translate the definition of an arithmetic sequence into an example. Say the constant in question is 4. Then the numbers from n on will be $n, n+4, n+8, n+12, n+16$. Then, Roman numeral I gives $3n, 3n+12, 3n+24, 3n+36, 3n+48$. That's still an arithmetic sequence, just with a different starting number, now $3n$, and a bigger constant, now 12. It's only one example, but I can see it will be true for any constant. So I is in. Given the answer choices, that means we won't have to evaluate III. As for II, this will just change the constant from 4 to 2, so that will be an arithmetic sequence.

The correct answer is (D).

Each of 16 individuals is to be given an identifying code consisting of one or more distinct digits in ascending order. What is the minimum number of distinct digits needed to give each individual a unique code?

- 3
- 4
- 5
- 6
- 7

Unique Code System

Each of 16 individuals is to be given an identifying code consisting of one or more distinct digits in ascending order. What is the minimum number of distinct digits needed to give each individual a unique code?

- 3
- 4
- 5
- 6
- 7

Explanation

In this question, we need 16 distinct codes, made up of digits that must be in ascending order, though they apparently do not have to be consecutive. Looking at the answer choices and imagining the simple case of three digits, say 1, 2, and 3, we can make the following codes:

1, 2, 3, 12, 13, 23, 123

We generated 7 different codes out of that. Not bad: let's try 4 digits:

1, 2, 3, 4

12, 13, 14, 23, 24, 34

123, 234, 124, 134

That got us 14 codes. Not quite enough. But 5 digits will certainly be enough, because we have those 14, plus the exciting new codes 5, 15, 25, 35, 45, and we can stop there, because we have generated more than 16 distinct codes.

The correct answer is (C).

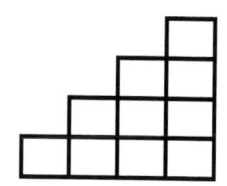

A stairway is formed by stacking even blocks next to and on top of each other. If the stairway depicted above is 5 blocks in length and 4 blocks in height, with a thin step at the beginning that does not require a block, and the stairway is only 1 block in width, how many blocks will be required to build such a stairway 20 blocks in length?

- 80
- 190
- 200
- 240
- 400

Stairway of Blocks

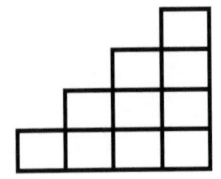

A stairway is formed by stacking even blocks next to and on top of each other. If the stairway depicted above is 5 blocks in length and 4 blocks in height, with a thin step at the beginning that does not require a block, and the stairway is only 1 block in width, how many blocks will be required to build such a stairway 20 blocks in length?

- 80
- 190
- 200
- 240
- 400

Explanation

In this question, the length of the stairway is padded by 1, because there is a block's length at the beginning with no blocks. In terms of blocks, it's really 19 blocks long. Received that way, the first unit of length is 1 block high, the second is 2 blocks high, and so on. So the number of blocks we need is

$$1 + 2 + 3 + \cdots + 17 + 18 + 19$$

We can find the sum of these numbers by using the average formula, since

$$\text{sum of items} = (\text{average of items})(\text{number of items})$$

The number of items we are adding is $19 - 1 + 1 = 19$, as we can confirm by playing with smaller numbers, if we have to. The average therefore will be the 10th item in the list, with 9 pairs of numbers on either side that balance the different out from that item. The tenth item is 10, so that's the average, and the sum is $(10)(19) = 190$. This is the number of blocks we need.

The correct answer is (B).

The height of Post A is 60 percent more than that of Post B, and the height of Post B is 60 percent less than that of Post C. What percent of Post C's height is Post A's height?

- 124%
- 120%
- 100%
- 80%
- 64%

Three Posts

The height of Post A is 60 percent more than that of Post B, and the height of Post B is 60 percent less than that of Post C. What percent of Post C's height is Post A's height?

- 124%
- 120%
- 100%
- 80%
- 64%

Explanation

Say Post B is 100 units tall. Post A is then 160 units tall. The height of post B is $(1 - 0.6) = 0.4$ times the height of Post C, so $100 = 0.4C$, and thus $C = \frac{100}{0.4}$. The percent of C's height that is A will be $\frac{A}{C} \times 100$, and this is

$$\frac{160}{\left(\frac{100}{0.4}\right)} \times 100\%$$

$$= \left(\frac{0.4}{0.4}\right) \frac{160}{\left(\frac{100}{0.4}\right)} \times 100\%$$

$$= \frac{(0.4)(160)}{100} \times 100\%$$

$$= (0.4)(1.60) = 64\%$$

The correct answer is (E).

Which of the following is equivalent to the pair of inequalities $y + 8 > 9$ and $y - 2 \leq 1$?

- $1 \leq y < 10$
- $1 \leq y < 4$
- $1 < y \leq 8$
- $1 < y \leq 3$
- $1 \leq y < 6$

Combining Inequalities II

Which of the following is equivalent to the pair of inequalities $y + 8 > 9$ and $y - 2 \leq 1$?

- $1 \leq y < 10$
- $1 \leq y < 4$
- $1 < y \leq 8$
- $1 < y \leq 3$
- $1 \leq y < 6$

Explanation

In this question, we can isolate y in each inequality:

$$y + 8 > 9$$

$$y > 1$$

So far, answer choices (A), (B), and (E) are out.

$$y - 2 \leq 1$$

$$y \leq 3$$

The correct answer is (D).

Albert has c coins, which is 4 times as many as Bob and $\frac{1}{3}$ as many as Candace. How many more coins do Bob and Candace have together than Albert does, in terms of c?

- $3c$
- $\frac{9}{4}c$
- $\frac{7}{4}c$
- $\frac{7}{3}c$
- $\frac{8}{3}c$

Albert's Coins

Albert has c coins, which is 4 times as many as Bob and $\frac{1}{3}$ as many as Candace. How many more coins do Bob and Candace have together than Albert does, in terms of c?

- $3c$
- $\frac{9}{4}c$
- $\frac{7}{4}c$
- $\frac{7}{3}c$
- $\frac{8}{3}c$

Explanation

In this question, we could pick the numbers for a case, but the algebra looks friendly, so we can write

$$c = 4b$$

$$c = \frac{1}{3}n$$

Where n stands for CaNdice, since Albert already has the variable c, contrary to intuitive naming. We want to obtain $n + b$, so we can multiply both equations and add them:

$$3c = 12b$$

$$36c = \left(\frac{1}{3}n\right)36 = 12n$$

$$12n + 12b = 39c$$

$$n + b = \frac{39c}{12} = \frac{13c}{4}$$

Bob and Candace have $\frac{13c}{4}$ coins, and Albert has c coins, so the difference is $\frac{9c}{4}$.

Another way to solve this question is to choose values. You can set $c = 12$, $b = 3$ and $N = 36$. The difference is $39 - 12 = 27$, which is indeed $\frac{9}{4}(12) = 9 \times 3$.

The correct answer is (B).

An operation Ω is defined by the equation $a\Omega b = \frac{-a-2b}{2a+b}$, for all numbers a and b such that $a \neq b$. If $a \neq -x$ and $\Omega x = 0$, then $x =$

- $-a$
- $-\frac{a}{2}$
- 0
- $\frac{a}{2}$
- a

Operation Omega

An operation Ω is defined by the equation $a\Omega b = \frac{-a-2b}{2a+b}$, for all numbers a and b such that $a \neq b$. If $a \neq -x$ and $\Omega x = 0$, then $x =$

- $-a$
- $-\frac{a}{2}$
- 0
- $\frac{a}{2}$
- a

Explanation

If $a\Omega x = 0$, then we apply the definition by plugging in x where b is and setting the result equal to 0:

$$a\Omega x = \frac{-a - 2x}{2a + x} = 0$$

We can multiply both sides by $2a + x$, and it vanishes.

$$-a - 2x = 0$$

$$-2x = a$$

$$x = -\frac{a}{2}$$

The correct answer is (B).

An animal that dives into a pool of water is at a depth of x, in feet, after t seconds, where $x = -4(t-2)^2 + 16$. At what depth, in feet, is the animal 0.5 seconds after it reaches its greatest depth?

- 7
- 12
- 15
- 16
- 17

Dive Into a Pool of Water

An animal that dives into a pool of water is at a depth of x, in feet, after t seconds, where $x = -4(t-2)^2 + 16$. At what depth, in feet, is the animal 0.5 seconds after it reaches its greatest depth?

- 7
- 12
- 15
- 16
- 17

Explanation

In this question, first we want to determine when the greatest depth happens. There are two terms in this expression for x; the first is positive, and the second is negative. The depth will be greatest when the negative term is smallest. That happens when $t = 2$, because then $(t-2)^2 = 0$. Note that $x = 16$ at this time, so after this time, the depth will be less, so answer choices (D) and (E) are out. So we want to know the depth when $t = 2.5$. That will be

$$x = -4(2.5 - 2)^2 + 16$$

$$x = -4\left(\frac{1}{2}\right)^2 + 16$$

$$x = -4\left(\frac{1}{4}\right) + 16 = -1 + 16 = 15$$

The correct answer is (C).

List A: 4, 7, 9, 14

List B: *m*, 2, 3, 9, 14

If the median of the numbers in list A above is equal to twice the median of the numbers in list B above, what is the value of *m*?

- 4
- 7
- 8
- 9
- 16

Comparing Medians

List A: 4, 7, 9, 14

List B: *m*, 2, 3, 9, 14

If the median of the numbers in list A above is equal to twice the median of the numbers in list B above, what is the value of *m*?

- 4
- 7
- 8
- 9
- 16

Explanation

In this question, the median of List A is 8, the average of 7 and 9. The median of List B is therefore 4. The only way for that to be the case is if *m* = 4.

The correct answer is (A).

For an exercise, 8 individuals must be assigned into pairs. How many different pairs can be assigned?

- 8
- 16
- 28
- 56
- 64

Assigning Pairs

For an exercise, 8 individuals must be assigned into pairs. How many different pairs can be assigned?

- 8
- 16
- 28
- 56
- 64

Explanation

In this question, let's imagine these 8 people lined up in a row, and imagine how we can pair them up. We can call the people A through H. There are seven ways to pair up person A with another person. That's true for each of the 8 people, so we have 8 × 7 = 56. But we have counted all the pairs twice. For example, 7 ways to find a pair for A counted AB, and 7 ways to find a pair for B counted BA. Therefore, we must divide by 2. The number of pairs is therefore 28. The correct answer is (C).

Another way to reach the answer starts the same: there are seven ways to choose a partner for A. Then, excluding the pair already counted, there are 6 ways to find a partner B that haven't been counted yet. There are 5 for C, and so on. So we have 7+6+5+4+3+2+1 =28 possibilities. This technique can be used for larger numbers also, because you can use the average formula to determine the sum of the numbers.

Again, the correct answer is (C).

At his regular hourly rate, Ed had estimated the cost of a research task as $528 and he was paid that amount. However, the job took 8 hours less time than he had estimated and, consequently, he earned $11 per hour more than his regular hourly rate. What was the time Ed took to complete the task, in hours?

- 36
- 25
- 16
- 8
- 4

Ed's Research Estimate

At his regular hourly rate, Ed had estimated the cost of a research task as $528 and he was paid that amount. However, the job took 8 hours less time than he had estimated and, consequently, he earned $11 per hour more than his regular hourly rate. What was the time Ed took to complete the task, in hours?

- 36
- 25
- 16
- 8
- 4

Explanation

We have friendly answer choices here, so we can try cases based on the answer choices. I'll start with (D), since it's easier to work with, and if I have to try (B) after (D), I should be able to infer the answer based on those two cases. If the task took 8 hours, then Ed had planned on 16 hours, that means that his normal rate must be

$$\frac{\$528}{16 \text{ hr}} = \$33/\text{hr}$$

He ended up earning $11 more than planned per hour, so that would be $43/hr. And $43 \times 8 = 344$, but that's supposed to add up to $528. So (D) is wrong. I would normally go to (B), but (D) was not that far off and (C) is going to be easier to compute, so let's try that. If the task took 16 hours, then the planned time was 24 hours, and Ed's rate is

$$\frac{\$528}{24 \text{ hr}} = \$22/\text{hr}$$

Does $33 \times 16 = 528$? Actually, yes; we already found that above. So (C) checks out.

The correct answer is (C).

The price of 15 purchased items was $316.80, including a 10 percent sales tax. What was the average price per purchased item, EXCLUDING the tax?

- $18.77
- $19.20
- $22.08
- $22.40
- $25.39

Average Excluding Tax

The price of 15 purchased items was $316.80, including a 10 percent sales tax. What was the average price per purchased item, EXCLUDING the tax?

- $18.77
- $19.20
- $22.08
- $22.40
- $25.39

Explanation

To compute the average of these 15 items *including* tax, we add up the prices and obtain $316.80, which we will then divide by 15. You can imagine all those pre-tax prices added up with the tax included: $1.1(x) + 1.1(y) + 1.1(z) + \cdots$. Whatever the prices are, the 1.1 can be factored out, so we have

$$\text{average of taxed prices} = \frac{(1.1)(\text{sum of pretax prices})}{15} = \frac{316.80}{15}$$

Therefore,

$$\frac{\text{sum of pretax prices}}{15} = \frac{316.80}{1.1(15)}$$

We can do a little long division to find $\frac{3168}{11}$

```
           2  8  8.
      11 | 3  1  6  8.
           2  2
           -----
              9  6
              8  8
              -----
                 8  8
                 8  8
                 -----
                    0
```

$288 is the sum of the pre-tax prices, so the average is $\frac{288}{15}$. We can perform a second long division and when we get $19 and change we can stop, since there is only one such answer. The correct answer is (B).

In a town, 25 percent of the population are miners by profession, and 16 percent of the population are employed miners. What percent of the miners in the town are not employed?

- 4%
- 12%
- 16%
- 25%
- 36%

Unemployed Miners

In a town, 25 percent of the population are miners by profession, and 16 percent of the population are employed miners. What percent of the miners in the town are not employed?

- 4%
- 12%
- 16%
- 25%
- 36%

Explanation

Let's say that 100 people live in Town X. That means we have 25 miners in the town, though they may not all be employed. Indeed, 16% or 16 people are employed miners. So the proportion of miners who are not employed is $\frac{25-16}{25} = \frac{9}{25} = \frac{36}{100}$.

The correct answer is (E).

If money is invested at r percent interest, compounded annually, the amount of the investment will double in approximately $\frac{70}{r}$ years. If Chris invests $1,000 in a bond that pays 4 percent interest, compounded annually, what will be the approximate total amount of the investment 35 years later?

- $4,000
- $2,200
- $2,000
- $1,800
- $1,200

Doubling Investment

If money is invested at r percent interest, compounded annually, the amount of the investment will double in approximately $\frac{70}{r}$ years. If Chris invests $1,000 in a bond that pays 4 percent interest, compounded annually, what will be the approximate total amount of the investment 35 years later?

- $4,000
- $2,200
- $2,000
- $1,800
- $1,200

Explanation

This question gives us a doubling formula and then some information to use it. The doubling time is $\frac{70}{r}$ and we are given $r = 4$, so the time to double is $\frac{70}{4} = \frac{35}{2} = 17.5$ years. We start with $1,000. It doubles to $2,000 in 17.5 years. In the next 17.5 years, it doubles to $4,000. The answer is (A). The doubling formula is handy to know, but notice that we were not expected to know it — it was given to us, and we were expected to know how to use it.

Again, the correct answer is (A).

A certain country has livestock numbering 6×10^8. If the population of the country is 12 million, what is the count of livestock per capita?

- 0.5
- 2
- 5
- 20
- 50

Livestock per Capita

A certain country has livestock numbering 6×10^8. If the population of the country is 12 million, what is the count of livestock per capita?

- 0.5
- 2
- 5
- 20
- 50

Explanation

This question expects us to know that "per capita" means "per person of the population." We can form a fraction. The "per" indicates the fraction bar, so livestock are on top and population on the bottom of the fraction:

$$\frac{6 \times 10^8}{12,000,000}$$

$$\frac{6 \times 10^8}{12 \times 10^6}$$

There are 8 10's in the numerator and 6 in the denominator, so 6 of them cancel:

$$\frac{6 \times 10^2}{12}$$

$$0.5 \times 100 = 50$$

The correct answer is (E).

If $\frac{r}{s} > 1$, and r and s are positive integers, which of the following must be less than 1?

- $\sqrt{\frac{r}{s}}$
- $\frac{r}{s^2}$
- $\frac{r}{2s}$
- $\frac{s^2}{r}$
- $\frac{s}{r}$

GFPS140

IMPROPER FRACTION

If $\frac{r}{s} > 1$, and r and s are positive integers, which of the following must be less than 1?

- $\sqrt{\frac{r}{s}}$
- $\frac{r}{s^2}$
- $\frac{r}{2s}$
- $\frac{s^2}{r}$
- $\frac{s}{r}$

EXPLANATION

If $\frac{r}{s} > 1$, then it's a so called improper fraction, such as $\frac{10}{9}$, or $\frac{33}{5}$. It means that $r > s$, as you can see by multiplying the inequality or considering cases. I give the answer choices a scan, and find (E) simplest and also correct. $\frac{s}{r}$ must be less than 1, as you can see from cases or by dividing $r > s$ by r.

The correct answer is (E).

It would take one machine 7 hours to complete a large production order and another machine 5 hours to complete the same order. If they can work on the order simultaneously without interfering with each other, how many hours would it take both machines, working simultaneously at their respective constant rates, to complete the order?

- $\frac{12}{35}$
- $1\frac{13}{35}$
- $2\frac{11}{12}$
- $5\frac{5}{7}$
- 12

Combined Rate of Two Machines

It would take one machine 7 hours to complete a large production order and another machine 5 hours to complete the same order. If they can work on the order simultaneously without interfering with each other, how many hours would it take both machines, working simultaneously at their respective constant rates, to complete the order?

- $\frac{12}{35}$
- $1\frac{13}{35}$
- $2\frac{11}{12}$
- $5\frac{5}{7}$
- 12

Explanation

The rates of these two machines, as measured in units of orders per hour, add to give the combined rate of their working together.

$$\frac{1 \text{ order}}{7 \text{ hr}} + \frac{1 \text{ order}}{5 \text{ hr}} = \frac{1 \text{ order}}{x \text{ hr}}$$

$$\frac{5}{35} + \frac{7}{35} = \frac{1}{x}$$

$$\frac{12}{35} = \frac{1}{x}$$

$$x = \frac{35}{12}$$

This value doesn't pop out in the answer choices, but

$$x = \frac{35}{12} = 2\frac{11}{12}$$

The correct answer is (C).

Many people prefer to memorize the formula for what we have just done as

$$T = \frac{AB}{A+B},$$

This formula is swift to use, but I recommend working with rates directly to be able to handle more difficult questions, and also to let units guide you and prevent accidentally flipping a fraction.

Again, the correct answer is (C).

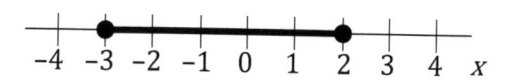

Which of the following inequalities is an algebraic expression for the shaded part of the number line above?

- $|x| \leq 2$
- $|x| \leq 3$
- $|x - 1| \leq 1$
- $\left|x - \frac{1}{2}\right| \leq \frac{5}{2}$
- $\left|x + \frac{1}{2}\right| \leq \frac{5}{2}$

Number Line Segment

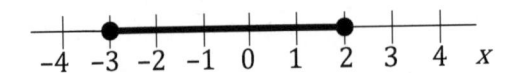

$$\begin{array}{c}\bullet\!\!-\!\!-\!\!-\!\!-\!\!-\!\!-\!\!-\!\!\bullet\\[-2pt]+\!\!-\!\!+\!\!-\!\!+\!\!-\!\!+\!\!-\!\!+\!\!-\!\!+\!\!-\!\!+\!\!-\!\!+\!\!-\!\!+\\[-2pt]-4\ -3\ -2\ -1\ \ 0\ \ 1\ \ 2\ \ 3\ \ 4\ \ x\end{array}$$

Which of the following inequalities is an algebraic expression for the shaded part of the number line above?

- ○ $|x| \leq 2$
- ○ $|x| \leq 3$
- ○ $|x - 1| \leq 1$
- ○ $\left|x - \frac{1}{2}\right| \leq \frac{5}{2}$
- ○ $\left|x + \frac{1}{2}\right| \leq \frac{5}{2}$

Explanation

The answer choices to this question indicate that we will deal with absolute value. Absolute value measures the distance of a quantity from zero. Here we have a slightly asymmetric situation. The line segment is 5 ticks long. If this line segment were centered on zero, it would be $|x| \leq \frac{5}{2}$. From that, we can see the answer must be (D) or (E). The term inside indicates the slight shift to the left. Which does it correctly? The center point of this line is $-\frac{1}{2}$; that's what we are measuring distance from in this expression, so if we put that in, we should get zero.

The correct answer is (E).

A legal service bills p dollars for the first hour of service on a task and q dollars for each additional hour, where $p > q$. If the client requires a specific number of hours h of service, how does the amount billed to the client change if the work is broken up into n tasks rather than one task?

- It increases by $p - q$ dollars
- It increases by $h(p - q)$ dollars
- It increases by $(n - 1)(p - q)$ dollars
- It decreases by $(h - 1)(p - q)$ dollars
- It decreases by $n(p - q)$ dollars

Legal Service Billing

A legal service bills p dollars for the first hour of service on a task and q dollars for each additional hour, where $p > q$. If the client requires a specific number of hours h of service, how does the amount billed to the client change if the work is broken up into n tasks rather than one task?

- It increases by $p - q$ dollars
- It increases by $h(p - q)$ dollars
- It increases by $(n - 1)(p - q)$ dollars
- It decreases by $(h - 1)(p - q)$ dollars
- It decreases by $n(p - q)$ dollars

Explanation

Imagining a case here helps understand the question even if we don't compute everything. The first hour costs more than the others – say it costs double. In that case, a 10-hour job, where $h = 10$, costs $p + 9q$. If we break it up into five jobs, two hours each it's $5(p + q) = 5p + 5q$. We can tell that it's going up, and that it depends on the number of jobs we are breaking it into, so (C) is the only possibility. We can, optionally, compute the difference in our case: $(5p + 5q) - (p + 9q) = 4p - 4q$. This corresponds to answer choice (C).

The correct answer is (C).

Chris' average (arithmetic mean) daily expenses were $500 per day over a 15-day trip. During this period, if Chris' average daily expenses were $450 for the first 5 days, what were the average daily expenses for the last 10 days?

- $505.00
- $515.00
- $525.00
- $532.50
- $550.00

Chris' Average Expenses

Chris' average (arithmetic mean) daily expenses were $500 per day over a 15-day trip. During this period, if Chris' average daily expenses were $450 for the first 5 days, what were the average daily expenses for the last 10 days?

- $505.00
- $515.00
- $525.00
- $532.50
- $550.00

Explanation

We can solve this question quickly with the knowledge that differences from the average in a group of numbers must net to zero. If the trip were 10 days, and the first 5 days were $450, then the last 5 days would average $550 for the overall balance to be $500. But there are twice as many days in the second group, so it carries twice as much weight. Therefore, it must be half as far from $500 to $550, or $525.

The correct answer is (C).

A certain rectangular window is half as long as it is wide. If its area is 20 feet, then its dimensions in feet are

- $\sqrt{10}$ by $\sqrt{10}$
- $\sqrt{5}$ by $\sqrt{2}$
- $2\sqrt{10}$ by $\sqrt{10}$
- $2\sqrt{5}$ by $\sqrt{10}$
- 6.66 by 3.33

Dimensions of a Window

A certain rectangular window is half as long as it is wide. If its area is 20 feet, then its dimensions in feet are

- $\sqrt{10}$ by $\sqrt{10}$
- $\sqrt{5}$ by $\sqrt{2}$
- $2\sqrt{10}$ by $\sqrt{10}$
- $2\sqrt{5}$ by $\sqrt{10}$
- 6.66 by 3.33

Explanation

The dimensions of this rectangle are x and $2x$. The area is therefore

$$2x^2 = 20$$

$$x^2 = 10$$

$$x = \sqrt{10}$$

Therefore the dimensions are $\sqrt{10}$ and $2\sqrt{10}$.

The correct answer is (C).

A company has 400 employees, 20 percent of whom have 5 or more years of work experience. If 40 additional employees are to be hired and all of the present employees remain, how many of the additional employees must have 5 or more years of work experience in order to raise the percent of employees with 5 or more years of work experience to 25 percent?

- 10
- 15
- 20
- 25
- 30

Increasing a Percent

A company has 400 employees, 20 percent of whom have 5 or more years of work experience. If 40 additional employees are to be hired and all of the present employees remain, how many of the additional employees must have 5 or more years of work experience in order to raise the percent of employees with 5 or more years of work experience to 25 percent?

- 10
- 15
- 20
- 25
- 30

Explanation

The algebra would not be too fearsome here, but the answer choices are nice square numbers virtually begging to be plugged into the question. We know 20% of 400 employees have this level of experience, so that's 80. We're going to hire 40 people, and x of them will have this experience, so

$$\frac{80 + x}{440} = 25\% = \frac{1}{4}$$

Therefore, x must be 30, to bring the numerator to 110 or $\frac{1}{4}$ of 440.

The correct answer is (E).

A quantity of substance weighing 2.83 milligrams, rounded to the nearest hundredth of milligram, was sold according to the latest market price, which was $18.66 per milligram, rounded to the nearest cent. The actual price used in this sale, in dollars per milligram, must have been between

- $\frac{18.66}{2.835}$ and $\frac{18.66}{2.825}$
- $\frac{18.665}{2.83}$ and $\frac{18.655}{2.83}$
- $\frac{18.655}{2.83}$ and $\frac{18.665}{2.83}$
- $\frac{18.655}{2.835}$ and $\frac{18.665}{2.825}$
- $\frac{18.665}{2.835}$ and $\frac{18.655}{2.825}$

Rounded Weight and Actual Weight

A quantity of substance weighing 2.83 milligrams, rounded to the nearest hundredth of milligram, was sold according to the latest market price, which was $18.66 per milligram, rounded to the nearest cent. The actual price used in this sale, in dollars per milligram, must have been between

- $\frac{18.66}{2.835}$ and $\frac{18.66}{2.825}$
- $\frac{18.665}{2.83}$ and $\frac{18.655}{2.83}$
- $\frac{18.655}{2.83}$ and $\frac{18.665}{2.83}$
- $\frac{18.655}{2.835}$ and $\frac{18.665}{2.825}$
- $\frac{18.665}{2.835}$ and $\frac{18.655}{2.825}$

Explanation

We have two rounded quantities in a rate. The value 2.83 has been rounded, so the actual value could be lower or higher. Ditto for 18.66. To determine the lowest fraction of the two, we take the least possible numerator and the greatest possible denominator. The bottom limit for the numerator is 18.655 and the upper limit for the denominator is 2.835, so that's the lowest fraction. Only (D) has that correct. We double check that the second fraction has the inverse logic.

The correct answer is (D).

If the operation ⊕ is defined by $x \oplus y = y\sqrt{x}$ for all positive numbers x and y, then $9 \oplus (16 \oplus 25) =$

- 60
- 180
- 240
- 300
- 1200

Custom Operation

If the operation $\oplus$ is defined by $x \oplus y = y\sqrt{x}$ for all positive numbers x and y, then $9 \oplus (16 \oplus 25) =$

- 60
- 180
- 240
- 300
- 1200

Explanation

In this question, we are given the definition of an operation that has been created just for the purpose of the question. To evaluate the given expression, we will apply the definition. Parentheses have not been given any special definition here, so we will take them to have their usual meaning, which is that we perform the operation inside the parentheses first, and use the result to perform the operation a second time.

$$16 \oplus 25 = 25\sqrt{16} = 25(4) = 100$$

So, applying the definition again:

$$9 \oplus (16 \oplus 25) = 9 \oplus 100 = 100\sqrt{9} = 300$$

The correct answer is (D).

A purchase cost $27.50 before tax. If the tax on the purchase was more than 10 percent but less than 15 percent of the cost of the purchase before tax, then the total amount paid must have been between

- $31 and $33
- $30 and $32
- $29 and $31
- $28 and $30
- $27 and $29

Percentage to Range Estimate

A purchase cost $27.50 before tax. If the tax on the purchase was more than 10 percent but less than 15 percent of the cost of the purchase before tax, then the total amount paid must have been between

- $31 and $33
- $30 and $32
- $29 and $31
- $28 and $30
- $27 and $29

Explanation

In this question, we'll consider two cases. First, say the tax was 10 percent. Technically, this is not allowed, but it's a limiting case. In that case the tax was $(0.1)27.50 = 2.75$ and the total purchase would be $27.50 + 2.75 = \$30.25$. In the limiting case on the upper half, the tax is 50% greater, so it's $2.75 \times \frac{3}{2} = 2\frac{3}{4} \times \frac{3}{2} = \frac{11}{4} \times \frac{3}{2} = \frac{33}{8} = 4\frac{1}{8} = \$4.125$. Then the total would be $\$27.50 + 4.125 = \$31.625$. So the total must be between $30.25 and $31.625. The range points of the correct answer can be exactly these, or they can be more expansive, but they cannot be narrower on either side. In other words, the interval we have identified must be contained with the correct answer.

The correct answer is (B).

If <n> is the greatest integer less than or equal to n, what is the value of (< −2.1 >)(< 2.1 >)(< 2.9 >) ?

- 2
- 0
- −8
- −12
- −18

Definition: Less Than or Equal To

If <n> is the greatest integer less than or equal to n, what is the value of $(< -2.1 >)(< 2.1 >)(< 2.9 >)$?

- 2
- 0
- -8
- -12
- -18

Explanation

Here we are given a definition for the pair of pointy brackets, a definition which is unique to this question. <n> is less than n but the greatest value possible, "possible" meaning that it must be an integer. Crudely, it's like, "barely less than n, rounded." So the barely-less-than-n-rounded number for $< -2.1 >$ is -3, as it's the integer just left of -2.1 on the number line. Actually, that's a better paraphrasal: the integer just left on the number line. We have

$$(< -2.1 >)(< 2.1 >)(< 2.9 >)$$

$$(-3)(2)(2) = -12$$

The correct answer is (D).

On a fishing expedition, the total weight of Eduardo's two heaviest catches was 30 pounds. If twice the weight of the first of those catches was 12 pounds more than the weight of the second of them, what was the weight, in pounds, of the first of them?

- 9
- 11
- 13
- 14
- 16

Eduardo's Heaviest Catches

On a fishing expedition, the total weight of Eduardo's two heaviest catches was 30 pounds. If twice the weight of the first of those catches was 12 pounds more than the weight of the second of them, what was the weight, in pounds, of the first of them?

- 9
- 11
- 13
- 14
- 16

Explanation

We're only talking about two catches here. We can call their weights A and B. Plugging numbers and algebra are about equally viable here, in my view. We are told that

$$A + B = 30$$

And

$$2A = B + 12$$

We want A, because it's "the first of them." We can get that quickly by adding the equations:

$$3A + B = B + 42$$

$$3A = 42$$

$$A = 14$$

The correct answer is (D).

At an archeological ruins site, flat tile fragments are discovered that have a collective surface area of 298 square feet. If the area of each fragment is at least 15 square feet, what is the greatest number of fragments that could be present in the discovery?

- 17
- 18
- 19
- 20
- 21

Surface Area of Tile Fragments

At an archeological ruins site, flat tile fragments are discovered that have a collective surface area of 298 square feet. If the area of each fragment is at least 15 square feet, what is the greatest number of fragments that could be present in the discovery?

- 17
- 18
- 19
- 20
- 21

Explanation

In this question, we want to know the greatest number of fragments possible. The greatest number of fragments means the smallest fragments, so we can have more of them. If we had 20 fragments each of the minimum size, the total would be 15 × 20 = 300 square feet. That is 2 square feet too many. So we can take away one fragment and we have 19. If they are all the minimum size, then that covers 300 − 15 = 285 square feet. But there isn't an upper limit on the sizes, so we could have 18 minimum-size fragments and one big fragment to cover the difference. So 20 is too many, while 19 is possible. Therefore, 19 is the maximum.

The correct answer is (C).

If x is the smallest positive integer such that 485,100 divided by x is twice the square of an integer, then x must be

- 2
- 11
- 22
- 77
- 105

Divisibility by Twice a Square

If x is the smallest positive integer such that 485,100 divided by x is twice the square of an integer, then x must be

- 2
- 11
- 22
- 77
- 105

Explanation

To make sense of this question, we are going to need the prime factorization of 485,100.

$$485{,}100 = 4851 \times 100$$

$$= 3(1617) \times 100$$

$$= 3(3)(539) \times 100$$

Both of these two steps were made possible by seeing the digits summed to 3, so the number had to be divisible by 3. It's the first thing to check after checking whether a number is even.

Working up, for 539, 3 doesn't work, 5 doesn't work, but

$$= 3(3)(7)(77) \times 100$$

$$= 3(3)(7)(7)(11) \times (2)(5)(2)(5)$$

$$= 2^2 3^2 5^2 7^2 11$$

This result is the original number expressed in its prime factorization. We are looking for a number x such that $\frac{2^2 3^2 5^2 7^2 11}{x}$ is twice the square of some integer. We can construct twice the square of an integer from these factors as $2(3 \times 5 \times 7)^2$. The number $(3 \times 5 \times 7)^2$ is a square, so the number $2(3 \times 5 \times 7)^2$ is twice a square. Moreover, it's the largest possible double of a square out of the factors $2^2 3^2 5^2 7^2 11$. We are using as many of the factors as possible, so x can be as small as possible, per the question. And x has to cancel the rest, so $x = 2 \times 11 = 22$. We've found that 22 is the smallest number that we can put in the denominator and get 2 times the square of an integer up top.

The correct answer is (C).

On average, each member of Team B earned $\frac{3}{5}$ as much as each member of Team A last year. If Team B has $\frac{3}{4}$ as many members as Team A, what fraction of the total earnings did Team A earn?

- $\frac{1}{2}$
- $\frac{7}{12}$
- $\frac{3}{5}$
- $\frac{5}{8}$
- $\frac{20}{29}$

Earnings per Team and per Member

On average, each member of Team B earned $\frac{3}{5}$ as much as each member of Team A last year. If Team B has $\frac{3}{4}$ as many members as Team A, what fraction of the total earnings did Team A earn?

- $\frac{1}{2}$
- $\frac{7}{12}$
- $\frac{3}{5}$
- $\frac{5}{8}$
- $\frac{20}{29}$

Explanation

This question is not unduly difficult to examine through a case. It's even easier if we work it backwards. Team B has $\frac{3}{4}$ as many members. Say Team A has 100 people and Team B has 75. Each person on Team A earned $10 (it's not a very high-performing team) and each person on Team B earned $6. This case fits all the parameters given. The total earnings will be

$$100(\$10) + 75(\$6)$$

And the fraction of the total earnings that Team A earned is

$$\frac{100(\$10)}{100(\$10) + 75(\$6)}$$

$$\frac{100(\$10)}{100(\$10) + 75(\$6)} \times \frac{\frac{1}{100}}{\frac{1}{100}}$$

$$\frac{10}{10 + \frac{3}{4}(6)}$$

$$\frac{10}{10 + \frac{9}{2}}$$

$$\frac{10}{10 + \frac{9}{2}} \times \frac{2}{2} = \frac{20}{29}$$

Therefore, the correct answer is (E).

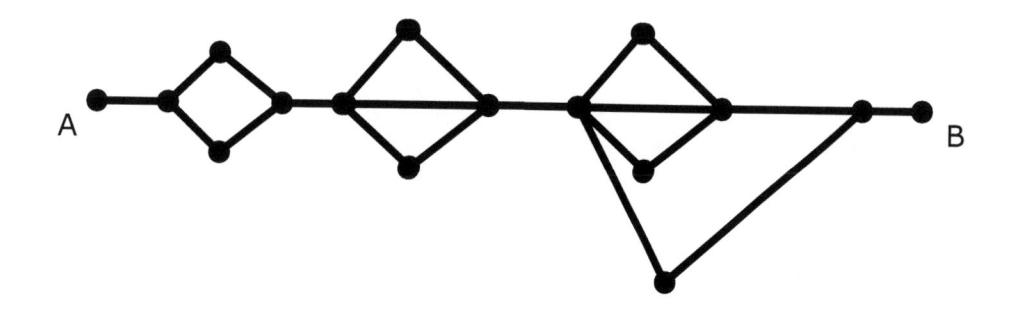

In the schematic diagram above, each point or line represents an answer to a survey question, which proceeds from left to right. How many different ways are there to proceed from Point A to Point B?

- 12
- 16
- 24
- 36
- 60

Possible Answers to a Survey

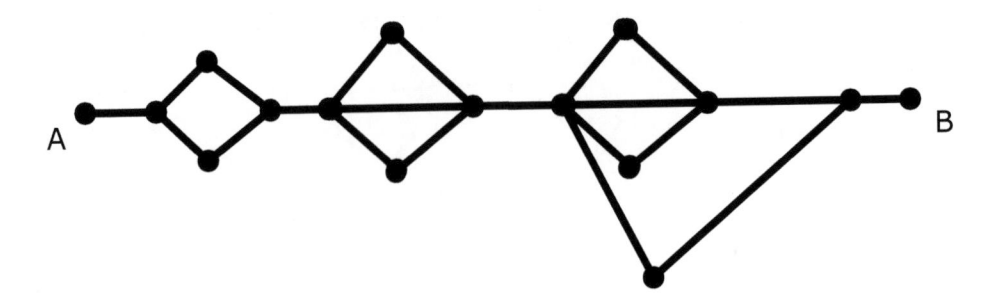

In the schematic diagram above, each point or line represents an answer to a survey question, which proceeds from left to right. How many different ways are there to proceed from Point A to Point B?

- 12
- 16
- 24
- 36
- 60

Explanation

This question has a particular diagram about a survey, but you could think of it as a schematic for a type of counting, permutation, and/or probability exercise that crops up on GMAT questions. The key here is that certain junctures are independent of others. For example, there are two ways to take the first fork. Looking past that, there is a juncture that can be traversed by top, middle or bottom. Whether we take top, middle, or bottom at that juncture is completely unaffected by whether we took the top or bottom path at the first juncture. For that reason, there are three ways to take the middle juncture *for each* of the two ways of taking the first juncture. In this context, "for each" is a key phrase hinting at multiplication. For that reason, there are 2 × 3 ways of getting past the second juncture (including getting past the first). There are four ways of crossing the final juncture, so the number of paths is 2 × 3 × 4 = 24.

The correct answer is (C).

A bar over a sequence of digits in a decimal indicates that the sequence repeats indefinitely. What is the value of $\frac{0.00\overline{16}}{0.\overline{04}}$?

- 0.04
- $0.\overline{04}$
- 0.4
- $0.\overline{4}$
- 400

Fraction with Repeating Decimals

A bar over a sequence of digits in a decimal indicates that the sequence repeats indefinitely. What is the value of $\frac{0.00\overline{16}}{0.\overline{04}}$?

- 0.04
- $0.\overline{04}$
- 0.4
- $0.\overline{4}$
- 400

Explanation

In this question, the zeroes on the top of the fraction are a little different than under the fraction, because the zeroes in the numerator do not repeat. So we can write

$$\frac{0.\overline{16}}{0.\overline{04}} \times 10^{-2}$$

To simplify the fraction, forget about the horizontal bars for a second. The fraction $\frac{0.16}{0.04}$ is 4. The fraction $\frac{0.1616}{0.0404}$ is also 4. And so on. Since both the 16 and the 04 are infinitely repeating in equal measure, the fraction is just 4. So

$$\frac{0.\overline{16}}{0.\overline{04}} \times 10^{-2} = 4 \times 10^{-2} = 0.04$$

The correct answer is (A).

A final note: you may be surprised to hear that the decimals above can be converted into fractions. You may be aware that a digit over 9 equals that digit repeating in decimal form: $\frac{1}{9} = 0.\overline{1}, \frac{2}{9} = 0.\overline{2}$, and the classic example, $\frac{3}{9} = 0.\overline{3} = \frac{1}{3}$. Note that $\frac{1}{9}$ is the same as $\frac{11}{99}$. In fact, any two-digit number over 99 is that two-digit sequence repeating. So the fraction $\frac{0.\overline{16}}{0.\overline{04}}$ is actually $\frac{16}{99}$ divided by $\frac{4}{99}$. The 99's cancel, and we are left with $\frac{16}{4} = 4$. No GMAT question will ever expect you to know this fact, but it can be handy occasionally (and division by 9 is quite likely to come in handy at least once on test day) when trying to simplify computations.

Again, the correct answer is (A).

On January first, Jamie did 1 sit-up. On each of the next 364 days, she did 1 more sit-up than on the preceding day. What was the total number of sit-ups she did over the 365 days?

- 66,430
- 66,795
- 66,978
- 67,160
- 132,860

Sum of Sit-Ups Over a Year

On January first, Jamie did 1 sit-up. On each of the next 364 days, she did 1 more sit-up than on the preceding day. What was the total number of sit-ups she did over the 365 days?

- 66,430
- 66,795
- 66,978
- 67,160
- 132,860

Explanation

To compute a sum of consecutive integers, we can use the average formula. You may know a formula for the sum of consecutive integers; it's actually derived from the average formula. From the average formula, we have

$$\text{sum of items} = (\text{average of items})(\text{number of items})$$

In this case, we are summing numbers from $1 + 2 + 3 + \cdots + 363 + 364 + 365$. The number of items in this list is $365 - 1 + 1 = 365$, the difference of the first and the last, plus 1. The average will be the middle number. We have $\frac{364}{2} = 182$ numbers below this number and 182 numbers above this number, so it's the 183rd number and is equal to 183. On other side of 183, there is a pair of equally spaced numbers that cancel the offset from 183, indicating that itsss is in fact the mean of all the numbers, not just the median. Therefore,

$$\text{sum of items} = (183)(365)$$

This is a little on the unfriendlier side of what we'd be expected to calculate on the GMAT. We can multiply these directly, or break one into factors and do successive smaller multiplications. Actually, on that note, we can see that this product must be divisible by 3, from the first term, and 5, from the second term. Comparing that with the answer choices: (C) is out, because it is not divisible by 5. Then, (A) is out because $6 + 6 + 4 + 3 + 0 = 19$, which is not divisible by 3. And (D) is out, because $6 + 7 + 1 + 6 + 0 = 20$, which is not divisible by 3. In (E), $1 + 3 + 2 + 8 + 6 + 0 = 20$, which is not divisible by 3. So we can actually rule out all the other answer choices based on divisibility rules. If we compute directly, we'll find that the product is indeed 66,795.

The correct answer is (B).

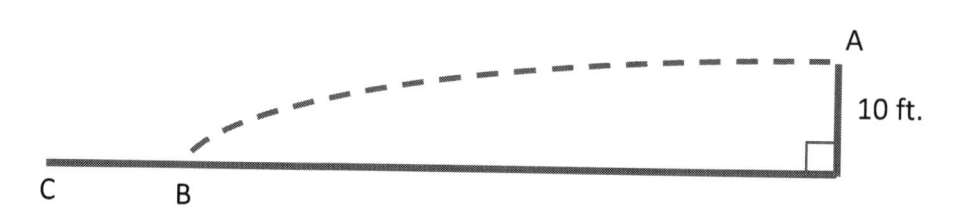

A projectile is fired at a target at point C, which lies 100 feet from the base of the platform from which the projectile was fired at point A. If AB = 90 feet, by what distance, in feet, did the projectile fall short of its target?

- $100 - 40\sqrt{5}$
- $100 - 40\sqrt{3}$
- 20
- 25
- 40

A Projectile Falls Short

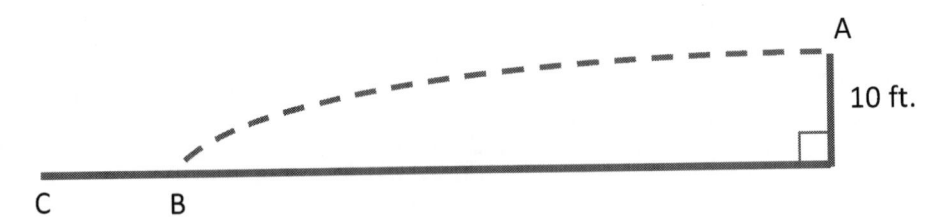

A projectile is fired at a target at point C, which lies 100 feet from the base of the platform from which the projectile was fired at point A. If AB = 90 feet, by what distance, in feet, did the projectile fall short of its target?

- $100 - 40\sqrt{5}$
- $100 - 40\sqrt{3}$
- 20
- 25
- 40

Explanation

The arc of the projectile is merely a distraction to what we will use in this question, which is a triangle. The height of the triangle is 10, the hypotenuse (from A to B) is 90, and the base B is the actual distance traveled by the projectile (which is somewhat less than the intended distance to point C, which is 100). By the Pythagorean Theorem, we have

$$90^2 = B^2 + 10^2$$

$$8100 = B^2 + 100$$

$$B^2 = 8000$$

$$B = \sqrt{8000} = \sqrt{80 \times 100} = 10\sqrt{80} = 10\sqrt{(16)(5)} = 40\sqrt{5}$$

The difference between this and the intended distance of 100 is the distance by which the projectile fell short.

The correct answer is (A).

Frederique traveled $\frac{x}{8}$ of the total distance of a trip at an average speed of 40 miles per hour, where $1 \leq x \leq 7$. She traveled the rest of the distance at an average speed of 60 miles per hour. In terms of x, what was Frederique's average speed for the entire trip?

- $\frac{180-x}{2}$
- $\frac{x+60}{4}$
- $\frac{300-x}{8}$
- $\frac{800}{120-x}$
- $\frac{960}{x+16}$

FREDERIQUE'S TRIP

Frederique traveled $\frac{x}{8}$ of the total distance of a trip at an average speed of 40 miles per hour, where $1 \leq x \leq 7$. She traveled the rest of the distance at an average speed of 60 miles per hour. In terms of x, what was Frederique's average speed for the entire trip?

- $\frac{180-x}{2}$
- $\frac{x+60}{4}$
- $\frac{300-x}{8}$
- $\frac{800}{120-x}$
- $\frac{960}{x+16}$

EXPLANATION

We can use a combination of analysis by cases and algebra. If $x = 4$, she traveled half the distance at 40 miles per hour and half the distance at 60 miles per hour. The average distance will be total distance divided by total time. Let's call the total distance D. Then the partial distances are $\frac{4}{8}D$ and $\frac{4}{8}D$, and the corresponding times are $\frac{\frac{4}{8}D}{40}$ and $\frac{\frac{4}{8}D}{60}$ so:

$$\text{average speed} = \frac{D}{\frac{\frac{4}{8}D}{40} + \frac{\frac{4}{8}D}{60}}$$

The D's cancel out; the total distance has no bearing on the answer.

$$= \frac{1}{\frac{\frac{4}{8}}{40} + \frac{\frac{4}{8}}{60}}$$

We can see that x affects the share of eighths that go over the 40 in this denominator versus over the 60. We can cancel all fractions except one by multiplying top and bottom by 8 and 120:

$$= \frac{1}{\frac{\frac{4}{8}}{40} + \frac{\frac{4}{8}}{60}} \times \frac{120}{120} \times \frac{8}{8} = \frac{(8)(120)}{(3)(4) + 2(4)}$$

The 4's correspond to x and $8 - x$. We can plug them back in:

$$= \frac{(8)(120)}{3x + 2(8-x)} = \frac{(8)(120)}{x + 16}$$

The correct answer is (E).

If $x = (103)^{103} + (3)^{95}$, what is the units digit of x?

- 0
- 1
- 2
- 3
- 4

Units Digit of an Exponent

If $x = (103)^{103} + (3)^{95}$, what is the units digit of x?

- 0
- 1
- 2
- 3
- 4

Explanation

In this question, one idea is to attempt to harmonize these terms into a single exponent, such as by finding a common base. But 103 is not divisible by 3. Another approach is to try to figure out the units digit of each term individually and then see what they must sum to. Evidently they will reliably sum to a particular digit, since the question has a particular answer.

We can look at cases of powers of 3:

1: 3

2: 9

3: 27

4: 81

5: 243

6: $243 \times 3 = 600 + 120 + 9 = 729$

We can speculate, then confirm by imagining further multiplication, that we have a repeating sequence, since got back to a final digit of 3, which yields 9, as before, which will yield 7, as before, and so on. There are four different possible digits: 3, 9, 7, and 1. For this high powers, we need to count and figure out which one each lands on. In the second term, the 95th power goes through the cycle $\frac{95}{4} = 23\frac{3}{4}$ times. Namely, $23 \times 4 = 80 + 12 = 92$ times goes through 3, 9, 7, 1 an even number of times. Then we have 93, 94, and 95, which lands us on 7. The first term, by similar logic, lands us on a 7. So the sum of these two numbers will involve adding two units digits of 7, which will result in a units digit of 4.

The correct answer is (E).

If $\frac{4-2y}{2+y} = y$, what is the value of $y^2 + 4y + 4$?

- -4
- -1
- 0
- 1
- 8

Value of Quadratic Expression

If $\frac{4-2y}{2+y} = y$, what is the value of $y^2 + 4y + 4$?

- -4
- -1
- 0
- 1
- 8

Explanation

In this question, we might be able to reformat the equation on the left in order to obtain the equation on the right. If we cross-multiply we obtain

$$\frac{4-2y}{2+y} = y$$

$$4 - 2y = 2y + y^2$$

Moving everything to one side:

$$y^2 + 4y - 4 = 0$$

This is not quite what we wanted, as we need 4 to be positive, not negative. If we add 8 to both sides of the equation, we get

$$y^2 + 4y + 4 = 8$$

The left side is what we are asked for, and the right side tells us what it is. The correct answer is (E).

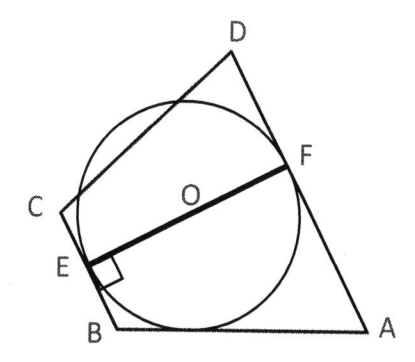

In the figure above, *EF* is a diameter of the circle with center *O* and is tangent at each end to the trapezoid *ABCD*. If the area of the circle is 225π, the length of *AD* is 20 and the length of *BC* is 10, what is the area of the *ABCD*?

- 432
- 440
- 450
- 460
- 470

Trapezoid and Circle

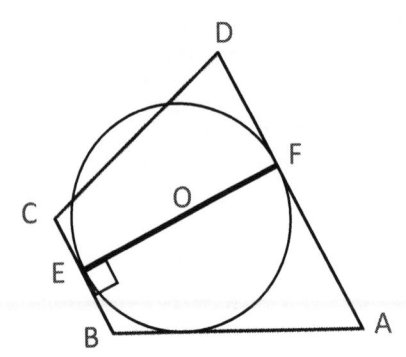

In the figure above, *EF* is a diameter of the circle with center *O* and is tangent at each end to the trapezoid *ABCD*. If the area of the circle is 225π, the length of *AD* is 20 and the length of *BC* is 10, what is the area of the *ABCD*?

- 432
- 440
- 450
- 460
- 470

Explanation

This diagram is a little strange, but we want the area of the trapezoid and we are given all the pieces to find it. Both bases of the trapezoid are given to us directly, and the height can be inferred from the area of the circle. Using the circle area formula:

$$225\pi = \pi r^2,$$

So $r = 15$. That means that the height of the trapezoid will be the diameter, which is 30. The area of a trapezoid is the height times the average of the bases (you can think of averaging the bases as computing the base of an equivalent rectangle), so

$$A = \frac{1}{2}(b_1 + b_2)h = \frac{1}{2}(20 + 10)(30) = 15(30) = 450$$

The correct answer is (C).

If $x = -1$, then $x^4 - x^3 + x^2 - x^1 + x^0 =$

- −3
- −2
- 3
- 4
- 5

Powers of Negative 1

If $x = -1$, then $x^4 - x^3 + x^2 - x^1 + x^0 =$

- ○ -3
- ○ -2
- ○ 3
- ○ 4
- ○ 5

Explanation

This question can be computed directly, knowing that negative numbers turn positive in pairs, and so will be positive when taken to even exponents and negative when taken to odd powers. Also, when dealing with negative signs, we can proceed with organization and confidence by putting everything first in parentheses.

$$(x^4) - (x^3) + (x^2) - (x^1) + (x^0)$$

$$(1) - (-1) + (1) - (-1) + (1)$$

$$1 + 1 + 1 + 1 + 1 = 5$$

The correct answer is (E).

By the way, if the zeroth power puzzles you, consider this. In the fraction $\frac{3^5}{3^4}$, the four 3's that are common to the numerator and denominator cancel, leaving the difference, $\frac{3^5}{3^4} = 3^{5-4} = 3^1$. Similarly, in the case of $\frac{3^4}{3^5}$, the same thing happens, but the extra three is left in the denominator: so $\frac{3^4}{3^5} = \frac{1}{3} = 3^{4-5} = 3^{-1}$. This provides a concrete example of why it makes sense that negative exponents correspond to positive exponents in the denominator. Secondly, it provides a concrete example of why we subtract the exponents when we have exponents of the same base in the numerator and the denominator. Finally, in the case of $\frac{3^5}{3^5}$, the number of 3's is five up top and on the bottom, so everything will cancel, yielding $\frac{3^5}{3^5} = 3^{5-5} = 3^0 = 1$. Since the base 3 is not material to these outcomes and could be replaced by any number or a variable, we have made a mini-proof of why these exponent properties are true and make sense.

Again, the correct answer is (E).

In a certain sequence, the term x_n is given by the formula $x_n = (x_{n-1})^2 + x_{n-2}$ for all $n \geq 2$. If $x_0 = 2$ and $x_1 = 3$, what is the value of x_3?

- 121
- 124
- 169
- 182
- 196

Recursive Sequence

In a certain sequence, the term x_n is given by the formula $x_n = (x_{n-1})^2 + x_{n-2}$ for all $n \geq 2$. If $x_0 = 2$ and $x_1 = 3$, what is the value of x_3?

- 121
- 124
- 169
- 182
- 196

Explanation

In this question, we must first glean that the value of a number of this sequence depends on the two prior values (in other words, it's recursive). That's what the subscript notation is telling us. We want x_3, but we don't have x_2, so we must first find x_2. Applying the definition,

$$x_2 = (x_1)^2 + x_0$$

$$= 3^2 + 2 = 11$$

Now we apply the definition again to get x_3:

$$x_3 = (x_2)^2 + x_1$$

$$= 11^2 + 3 = 121 + 3 = 124$$

The correct answer is (B).

A rectangle measuring 6 inches by 7 inches is centered inside a larger rectangle of proportional dimensions so that the perimeters of the two rectangles are separated by a uniform distance of x inches. If the difference between the areas of the two rectangles is 168 square inches, what is x?

- 3
- 4
- 6
- 8
- 9

Nested Rectangles

A rectangle measuring 6 inches by 7 inches is centered inside a larger rectangle of proportional dimensions so that the perimeters of the two rectangles are separated by a uniform distance of x inches. If the difference between the areas of the two rectangles is 168 square inches, what is x?

- 3
- 4
- 6
- 8
- 9

Explanation

In this question, we can see that the area of the lesser rectangle is 42, since it measures 6 by 7. We can draw a sketch:

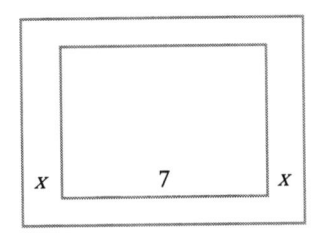

We can see that the width of the larger rectangle is $7 + 2x$. Similarly, the other dimension will be $6 + 2x$, and the area of the larger rectangle will be:

$$(7 + 2x)(6 + 2x)$$

This area minus the area of the smaller rectangle is 168, so

$$(7 + 2x)(6 + 2x) - 42 = 168$$

We can proceed by algebra or by answer-choice plugging. Let's try (B), $x = 4$:

$$(7 + 8)(6 + 8) - 42 = 168$$

$$(15)(14) - 42 = 168$$

$$210 - 42 = 168$$

This fits, so indeed the correct answer is (B).

This question is well-suited for answer-plugging; not only are the answer choice numbers friendly to work with, but if an answer is not correct, it's clear whether we will need a bigger or smaller number, to make the bigger rectangle bigger or smaller. Nevertheless, the plugging goes most swiftly if our understanding is set up with the diagram and the equation. Again, the correct answer is (B).

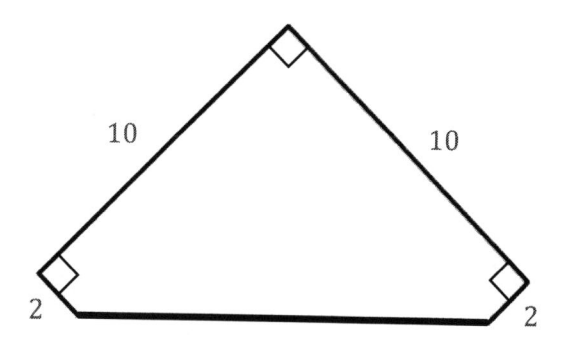

What is the area of the shape in the figure above?

- $40\sqrt{2}$
- 64
- 68
- 81
- 92

Area of Irregular Shape

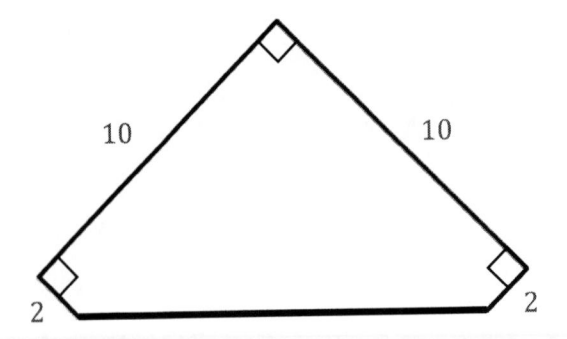

What is the area of the shape in the figure above?

- $40\sqrt{2}$
- 64
- 68
- 81
- 92

Explanation

This figure looks a bit like a trapezoid, but it's not a trapezoid: it has five sides, not four, and it doesn't have two parallel bases. It also resembles a rotated square that has been sliced; this resemblance will be more useful. Since there are three right angles and two equal sides, a square can be formed that contains this shape: the two short sides will have to intersect if we extend them, and they will have to form a right angle, since they are perpendicular to each other, meaning the extended shape is a square.

That means that the missing portion is a right triangle with sides 8 and 8. Those two sides are a valid base-height pair, so the area of that triangle is

$$\frac{1}{2}(8)(8) = (4)(8) = 32.$$

Meanwhile, the area of the square is $10^2 = 100$. The area of this shape in question is that of the square minus the area of the triangle, so it is

$$100 - 32 = 68.$$

The correct answer is (C).

A machine painting a room at a constant rate takes 6 hours to paint $\frac{5}{12}$ of the room. How much more time will it take to finish painting the room?

- 8 hr 10 min
- 8 hr 24 min
- 8 hr 30 min
- 8 hr 36 min
- 8 hr 42 min

A Painting Machine's Rate

A machine painting a room at a constant rate takes 6 hours to paint $\frac{5}{12}$ of the room. How much more time will it take to finish painting the room?

- 8 hr 10 min
- 8 hr 24 min
- 8 hr 30 min
- 8 hr 36 min
- 8 hr 42 min

Explanation

In this question, since the rate of this painting is constant, we can write a fraction for its rate painting so far and set it equal to the rate of the rest of the paining to be done:

$$\frac{\frac{5}{12} \text{ room}}{6 \text{ hours}} = \frac{\frac{7}{12} \text{ room}}{x \text{ hours}}$$

Cross-multiplying:

$$\frac{5}{12}x = \frac{7}{12}(6)$$

$$5x = 42$$

$$x = \frac{42}{5} = 8\frac{2}{5}$$

A fifth of an hour is $\frac{60}{5} = 12$ minutes, so the time remaining is 8 hours and 24 minutes. The correct answer is (B).

A positive number x is multiplied by 3, and this product is then divided by 4. If the square of the result of these two operations equals x, what is the value of x?

- $\frac{16}{9}$
- $\frac{4}{3}$
- $\frac{3}{2}$
- $\frac{3}{4}$
- $\frac{2}{3}$

Operations on Unknown Number

A positive number x is multiplied by 3, and this product is then divided by 4. If the square of the result of these two operations equals x, what is the value of x?

- $\frac{16}{9}$
- $\frac{4}{3}$
- $\frac{3}{2}$
- $\frac{3}{4}$
- $\frac{2}{3}$

Explanation

This question says:

$$\left(\frac{3x}{4}\right)^2 = x$$

$$\frac{9x^2}{16} = x$$

$$\frac{9}{16}x = 1$$

$$x = \frac{16}{9}$$

The correct answer is (A).

A tank contains 1,000 gallons of a solution that is 6 percent salt by volume. If 200 gallons of water evaporate from the tank, the remaining solution will be approximately what percent salt?

- 6.20%
- 7.00%
- 7.25%
- 7.50%
- 7.75%

Salt Solution

A tank contains 1,000 gallons of a solution that is 6 percent salt by volume. If 200 gallons of water evaporate from the tank, the remaining solution will be approximately what percent salt?

- 6.20%
- 7.00%
- 7.25%
- 7.50%
- 7.75%

Explanation

This question involves a ratio that changes. The ratio is in units of volume, volume of salt and volume of solution. Initially, we have

$$\frac{\text{salt}}{1{,}000} = \frac{6}{100}$$

$$\frac{\text{salt}}{1{,}000} = \frac{6}{100}\left(\frac{10}{10}\right) = \frac{60}{1{,}000}$$

So the initial volume of salt is 60. The final ratio will be the same volume of salt, with $1{,}000 - 200 = 800$ units of solution:

$$\frac{60}{800} = \frac{60}{800}\left(\frac{\frac{5}{4}}{\frac{5}{4}}\right) = \frac{60\left(\frac{5}{4}\right)}{1{,}000} = \frac{6\left(\frac{5}{4}\right)}{100}$$

The aim of this manipulation is to get the final ratio such that the denomination is 100, so we can pick off the numerator as the percent.

$$6\left(\frac{5}{4}\right) = \frac{30}{4} = \frac{15}{2} = 7.5$$

The correct answer is (D).

How many prime numbers between 1 and 30 are factors of 3,366?

- One
- Two
- Three
- Four
- Five

Counting Prime Number Factors

How many prime numbers between 1 and 30 are factors of 3,366?

- One
- Two
- Three
- Four
- Five

Explanation

To be ready for this question, we must have prime factorization always within arm's reach. First, we can express the number 3,366 in its prime factorization.

$$3,366$$

$$= 3(1122)$$

$$= 3(11)(102)$$

$$= 3(11)(2)(51)$$

$$= 3(11)(2)(3)(17)$$

$$= 2 \times 3^2 \times 11 \times 17$$

We have four distinct primes: 2, 3, 11, and 17. Therefore, there are four primes between 1 and 30 that are factors of 3,366.

The correct answer is (D).

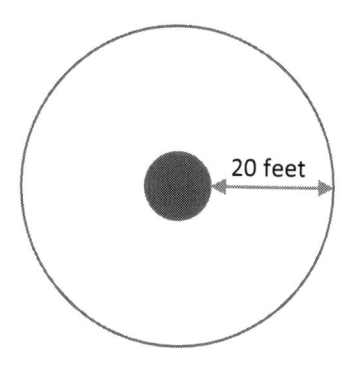

The ground within a circular garden and around the base of a circular statue exactly in its center, as shown in the figure above, is to be covered with gravel. If the base of the statue is 2 feet in diameter, how many square feet are to be covered with gravel?

- 324π
- 361π
- 399π
- 400π
- 440π

Circular Garden and Circular Statue

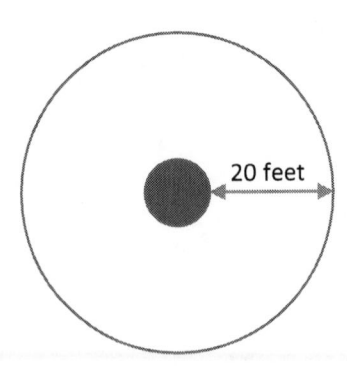

The ground within a circular garden and around the base of a circular statue exactly in its center, as shown in the figure above, is to be covered with gravel. If the base of the statue is 2 feet in diameter, how many square feet are to be covered with gravel?

- 324π
- 361π
- 399π
- 400π
- 440π

Explanation

The area to be covered with gravel is the area within the garden and not covered by the statue, so it will be the difference of these two areas. The radius of the statue is half the diameter, so it's 1. The radius of the large circle is 20 plus the radius of the statue, since the statue is in the center of the garden, so it's 21. Using $A = \pi r^2$ for the area of a circle, the small area is $A = \pi 1^2 = \pi$ and the larger area is $A = \pi(21)^2 = \pi(21)(21) = \pi(420 + 21) = 441\pi$. The difference is 440π.

The correct answer is (E).

John is now 10 years older than Janice. If 10 years ago John was twice as old as Janice, how old will John be in 5 years?

- 10
- 18
- 23
- 25
- 35

John's and Janice's Age

John is now 10 years older than Janice. If 10 years ago John was twice as old as Janice, how old will John be in 5 years?

- ○ 10
- ○ 18
- ○ 23
- ○ 25
- ○ 35

Explanation

In this question, the algebra translation commonly causes errors, but we can confirm the correct answer by walking it through the described scenario. If John's age is J and Janice's age is N, then

$$J = N + 10$$

and

$$J - 10 = 2(N - 10)$$

$$J - 10 = 2N - 20$$

$$J = 2N - 10$$

Substituting J:

$$N + 10 = 2N - 10$$

$$20 = N$$

And, plugging back into our topmost equation, $J = 30$. We confirm, 10 years ago, John was 20 and Janice was 10, so he was twice her age. We want John's age in 5 years, which is 35.

The correct answer is (E).

If $x = \frac{1}{2^2 \times 3^2 \times 4^2 \times 5^2}$ is expressed as a decimal, how many distinct nonzero digits will x have?

- One
- Two
- Three
- Seven
- Ten

Counting Nonzero Digits

If $x = \frac{1}{2^2 \times 3^2 \times 4^2 \times 5^2}$ is expressed as a decimal, how many distinct nonzero digits will x have?

- One
- Two
- Three
- Seven
- Ten

Explanation

In this question, we can separate the number x into two factors:

$$\frac{1}{3^2 \times 4^2} \times \frac{1}{10^2},$$

Since the latter portion is easy to add in afterward (and will contribute only digits of zero). Since $3^2 \times 4^2 = (3 \times 4)^2$, we have $\frac{1}{144}$. We can proceed by long division:

```
         0.  0  0  6  9  4
    144 | 1.  0  0  0  0  0  0  0
            8  8  4
            ─────────
            1  3  6  0
            1  2  9  6
            ─────────
                  6  4  0
                  5  7  6
                  ─────────
                        6  4  0
```

We have hit, finally, a situation in which the decimal will repeat: from here on out we'll have 4's. Therefore, the distinct non-zero digits in this decimal are 6, 9, and 4, for a grand total of 3.

The correct answer is (C).

What is the sum of all the odd integers between 100 and 302?

- 10,150
- 20,150
- 20,301
- 40,301
- 45,301

Sum of Many Odd Integers

What is the sum of all the odd integers between 100 and 302?

- 10,150
- 20,150
- 20,301
- 40,301
- 45,301

Explanation

When the GMAT says "sum," I think, "average." Indeed, we can use the reformatted average formula,

$$\text{sum of items} = (\text{average of items})(\text{number of items}).$$

The odd integers between 100 and 302 include 101, 103, … all the way up to 197 and 199, and then 201, 203, … all the way up to 299, and then a bonus at the end, 301. Counting both even and odd integers, the number of integers from 101 to 200 is $200 - 101 + 1 = 100$. Half of them are odd, so that first group has 50 odd numbers. So, altogether, we are talking about $50 + 50 + 1 = 101$ odd numbers, where the final one is the 301 at the end. Since they are evenly spaced, their average will be the median value. That will be the value 201, which will have 50 values below it and 50 above it. Therefore,

$$\text{sum of items} = (201)(101) = 201(100) + 201 = 20{,}100 + 201 = 20{,}301$$

The correct answer is (C).

A box contains b blue balls and r red balls. If 4 blue balls and 3 red balls are added to the box, and if one ball is obtained at random from the box, then the probability that a blue ball is obtained can be represented by

- $\dfrac{b}{r}$
- $\dfrac{b}{b+r}$
- $\dfrac{b+4}{r+3}$
- $\dfrac{b+4}{b+r+4}$
- $\dfrac{b+4}{b+r+7}$

The Probability of a Blue Ball

A box contains *b* blue balls and *r* red balls. If 4 blue balls and 3 red balls are added to the box, and if one ball is obtained at random from the box, then the probability that a blue ball is obtained can be represented by

- $\dfrac{b}{r}$
- $\dfrac{b}{b+r}$
- $\dfrac{b+4}{r+3}$
- $\dfrac{b+4}{b+r+4}$
- $\dfrac{b+4}{b+r+7}$

Explanation

If we get confused by the algebra here, or we are sick of algebra, we can pick the numbers for a specific case to test the answer choices, though I believe the algebraic method will be faster if your algebra is up to speed. The probability of drawing a blue ball will be the number of blue balls over the total number of balls. After we add the balls, the total number of balls is $b + r + 7$. (E) leaps out as the only viable answer choice, and indeed the number of blue balls is $b + 4$.

The correct answer is (E).

Last year the average health care cost per employee in Group G increased by *n* percent and the average compensation per employee in group G increased by *m* percent, where *n* is greater than *m*. By what percent did the ratio of health care cost per employee to compensation per employee increase, in terms of *n* and *m*?

- $\frac{n}{m}\%$
- $(n-m)\%$
- $\frac{100(n-m)}{100+n}\%$
- $\frac{100(n-m)}{100+m}\%$
- $\frac{100(n-m)}{100+n+m}\%$

Change in Health Care Cost per Employee

Last year the average health care cost per employee in Group G increased by n percent and the average compensation per employee in group G increased by m percent, where n is greater than m. By what percent did the ratio of health care cost per employee to compensation per employee increase, in terms of n and m?

- $\frac{n}{m}\%$
- $(n - m)\%$
- $\frac{100(n-m)}{100+n}\%$
- $\frac{100(n-m)}{100+m}\%$
- $\frac{100(n-m)}{100+n+m}\%$

Explanation

In this question, we are dealing with a ratio of two ratios. The overall ratio that we are interested in is

$$\frac{\left(\frac{\text{health cost}}{\text{employee}}\right)}{\left(\frac{\text{compensation}}{\text{employee}}\right)}$$

We can consider that the ratio for last year. This year, the top ratio increased by n percent and the bottom one increased by m percent, so this year's ratio is

$$\text{this year's ratio} = \frac{\left(1 + \frac{n}{100}\right)\left(\frac{\text{health cost}}{\text{employee}}\right)}{\left(1 + \frac{m}{100}\right)\left(\frac{\text{compensation}}{\text{employee}}\right)}$$

The question is asking us for a single percentage, call it x, by which the ratio increased. In other words,

$$1 + \frac{x}{100} = \frac{\left(1 + \frac{n}{100}\right)}{\left(1 + \frac{m}{100}\right)}$$

Would be the way to express the effect of n and m as a single percentage, x. Solving for x should give the answer. I'd be inclined to finish the algebra here, but I'm a little more algebra-leaning than most people. Let's consider a simple case, with values that may not be realistic but which are allowed and easy to compute. What if $m = 0$? Then $x = n$, because in that case there was no change the first year, and the overall rate of change was just the rate of change in the second year. We can apply that simple test to the answer choices. We can plug in $m = 0$ and see which cases give us n. Only (B) and (D). And (B) is clearly not equal to the above. So my love of algebra was unnecessary.

The correct answer is (D).

Of the 600 professionals who took an advanced certification examination, 50 percent passed the written portion of the exam, 30 percent passed the simulation portion of the exam, and 65 percent passed the demonstration portion of the exam. If 20 percent of the examinees passed no portion of the exam, and 35 percent of the subjects passed exactly two portions of the exam, how many of the subjects passed exactly one portion of the exam?

- 140
- 180
- 240
- 260
- 300

Portions of Advanced Certification

Of the 600 professionals who took an advanced certification examination, 50 percent passed the written portion of the exam, 30 percent passed the simulation portion of the exam, and 65 percent passed the demonstration portion of the exam. If 20 percent of the examinees passed no portion of the exam, and 35 percent of the subjects passed exactly two portions of the exam, how many of the subjects passed exactly one portion of the exam?

- 140
- 180
- 240
- 260
- 300

Explanation

This question pertains to three overlapping sets. It helps tremendously to be acquainted with the three-part Venn diagram and set (see the GMAT Free *Math Review* if you aren't), but the takeaway is that, as we are adding everything up, areas of overlap can get counted twice. If we add up the percentages of people who pass each of the parts and the people who passed none, we get

$$50\% + 30\% + 65\% + 20\% = 165\%,$$

Which is more than the number of people because some are double counted. We are told one of the double-counting areas: 35% of people passed exactly two areas. If we subtract that from 165% we are down to 130%. The difference is the number of people who have passed all three portions, and this portion is *triple*-counted, so we need to subtract it twice to count everyone once. That means 30% is twice the percentage who passed all three, which must therefore be 15%. Consequently, the percentage who passed exactly one will be the total minus those who passed neither, exactly two, and exactly three:

$$100\% - 20\% - 35\% - 15\% = 30\%$$

That number is 30% of 600, or 180. The correct answer is (B).

The positive integer k is divisible by 11. If $\sqrt{k}$ is greater than 11, which of the following could NOT be the value of $\frac{k}{11}$?

- 10
- 12
- 13
- 14
- 20

Impossible Value of K

The positive integer k is divisible by 11. If $\sqrt{k}$ is greater than 11, which of the following could NOT be the value of $\frac{k}{11}$?

- 10
- 12
- 13
- 14
- 20

Explanation

In this question, putting words into equations, we have

$$\frac{k}{11} = \text{integer},$$

Because that's what it means for k to be divisible by 11, and

$$\sqrt{k} > 11$$

$$k > (11)^2$$

Actually, since we want to know about $\frac{k}{11}$, we can reformat this last equation as

$$\frac{k}{11} > 11$$

Turns out we only needed the second fact, not the first. Among the answer choices, which are suggestions for $\frac{k}{11}$, only one stands out as disallowed, 10, because it's not greater than 11.

The correct answer is (A).

Items are sold by a retailer for a price of $30 each, which represents a 20 percent markup over the cost paid by the retailer for each item. Of 50 items ordered, 30 are sold, and 10 are returned to the manufacturer for a refund of 40 percent of the dealer's initial cost. If the remaining inventory is sold, what is the retailer's approximate profit or loss as a percent of the retailer's initial cost for the 50 items?

- 8% loss
- 4% loss
- 8% profit
- 4% profit
- 12% profit

Retailer's Profit on Items Ordered

Items are sold by a retailer for a price of $30 each, which represents a 20 percent markup over the cost paid by the retailer for each item. Of 50 items ordered, 30 are sold, and 10 are returned to the manufacturer for a refund of 40 percent of the dealer's initial cost. If the remaining inventory is sold, what is the retailer's approximate profit or loss as a percent of the retailer's initial cost for the 50 items?

- 8% loss
- 4% loss
- 8% profit
- 4% profit
- 12% profit

Explanation

In this question, the retailer's profit or loss as a percentage doesn't hinge on the $30 directly. He ends up selling 80% at 120% of the cost, the question asks us to assume. And he gets 40% of the cost as a refund on the other 20%. So, for the revenue, we can consider the cost 1 and construct a weighted average:

$$\text{revenue} = (0.8)(1.2) + (0.2)(0.4)$$

$$= 0.96 + 0.08$$

$$= 1.04$$

The "cost" is just 1, so the dealer has made a 4% profit. The correct answer is (D).

Note that, the more invested you get in doing calculations with the price of $30, the less likely you are to have chanced across this somewhat faster way of solving the question. No one finds the fastest way to solve a question every time, and you don't need to in order meet and beat your GMAT goal, whatever it is. But you do want to practice eyeing the question with a critical laziness before getting started in the interest of finding the straightest path.

Again, the correct answer is (D).

The employees at a company meeting are residents of the countries England, France, and Japan in the ratio 7:2:4, respectively. If 520 total employees are at the meeting, the meeting includes how many more residents of England than of Japan?

- 120
- 110
- 100
- 90
- 80

Employees from England and Japan

The employees at a company meeting are residents of the countries England, France, and Japan in the ratio 7:2:4, respectively. If 520 total employees are at the meeting, the meeting includes how many more residents of England than of Japan?

- 120
- 110
- 100
- 90
- 80

Explanation

In this question, the ratio 7:2:4 alone doesn't give us any absolute quantities, but they are in equal proportion, so we can think of each as multiplied by an integer n. Therefore, since the total is 520, we can write

$$7n + 2n + 4n = 520$$

$$13n = 520$$

$$n = 40$$

The difference between the number from England and from Japan will be $7n - 4n = 3n = 3(40) = 120$.

The correct answer is (A).

If $x^{-3} = -\frac{1}{8}$, then x^{-2} is equal to

- ○ -4
- ○ 4
- ○ $\frac{1}{4}$
- ○ $-\frac{1}{4}$
- ○ -2

Negative Exponents of Negative Fractions

If $x^{-3} = -\frac{1}{8}$, then x^{-2} is equal to

- -4
- 4
- $\frac{1}{4}$
- $-\frac{1}{4}$
- -2

Explanation-

In this question, we can write x^{-3} in the more intuitive format:

$$\frac{1}{x^3} = -\frac{1}{8}$$

That means that $x = -2$, which we can find by cross-multiplying and taking the cube root. Therefore, x^{-2} will be

$$\frac{1}{x^2} = \frac{1}{(-2)^2} = \frac{1}{4}.$$

The correct answer is (C).

If $k > 0$ and x is $2k$ percent of y, then, in terms of y, k is what percent of x?

- $50y$
- $\dfrac{1}{50y}$
- $\dfrac{2}{y}$
- $\dfrac{50}{y}$
- $\dfrac{5,000}{y}$

Percent of X

If $k > 0$ and x is $2k$ percent of y, then, in terms of y, k is what percent of x?

- $50y$
- $\dfrac{1}{50y}$
- $\dfrac{2}{y}$
- $\dfrac{50}{y}$
- $\dfrac{5{,}000}{y}$

Explanation

We use the word "is" in both statements to denote an equal sign. "x is $2k$ percent of y" becomes

$$x = \left(\frac{2k}{100}\right)y$$

We can confirm considering, "x is 80 percent of y." If we plug in the 80, it's correct. The statement we are looking for starts with "k is," or $k=$, so let's isolate k.

$$x = \frac{2ky}{100}$$

$$\frac{100}{2y}(x) = \left(\frac{2ky}{100}\right)\frac{100}{2y}$$

$$k = \left(\frac{100}{2y}\right)x$$

In order to be able to pluck a percent out of the portion in parentheses, the denominator must be 100. But it's $2y$, so we will multiply by a form of 1 that will make the denominator 100:

$$k = \frac{\frac{100}{2y}}{\frac{100}{2y}}\left(\frac{100}{2y}\right)x$$

$$k = \left(\frac{\frac{10{,}000}{2y}}{100}\right)x$$

It looks odd, but now the numerator of $\dfrac{10{,}000}{2y} = \dfrac{5{,}000}{y}$ is the answer. The variable k is $\dfrac{5{,}000}{y}\%$ of x.

The correct answer is (E).

Which of the following describes all values of x for which $1 - x^2 \leq 0$?

- $x \geq 1$
- $x \leq -1$
- $0 \leq x \leq 1$
- $x \leq -1$ or $x \geq 1$
- $-1 \leq x \leq 1$

Quadratic Inequality

Which of the following describes all values of x for which $1 - x^2 \leq 0$?

- $x \geq 1$
- $x \leq -1$
- $0 \leq x \leq 1$
- $x \leq -1$ or $x \geq 1$
- $-1 \leq x \leq 1$

Explanation

In this question, we have an inequality in which x is not isolated, so we can work to isolate it:

$$1 - x^2 \leq 0$$

$$1 \leq x^2$$

When we take the square root, there are two cases: x is positive, or x is negative.

Case I (positive): $1 \leq x$

Case II (negative): $-1 \geq x$

We can make sense of these results by considering that x is not a fraction with an absolute value of less than 1. Therefore, it must either be right of 1 on the number line or left of -1.

The correct answer is (D).

Carbon dioxide comprises, on average, about 397 parts per million of the Earth's atmosphere, on a molecular basis. In an even sample of the Earth's atmosphere consisting of 4 billion molecules, approximately how many of those molecules would be expected to be carbon dioxide? (1 billion = 1,000,000,000)

- 160,000
- 1,000,000
- 1,600,000
- 10,000,000
- 16,000,000

Molecules of Carbon Dioxide in a Sample

Carbon dioxide comprises, on average, about 397 parts per million of the Earth's atmosphere, on a molecular basis. In an even sample of the Earth's atmosphere consisting of 4 billion molecules, approximately how many of those molecules would be expected to be carbon dioxide? (1 billion = 1,000,000,000)

- 160,000
- 1,000,000
- 1,600,000
- 10,000,000
- 16,000,000

Explanation

In this question, we are working with a ratio that doesn't change, so we can write two instances of this ratio and set them equal:

$$\frac{397}{1{,}000{,}000} = \frac{x}{4{,}000{,}000{,}000}$$

Counting zeroes:

$$\frac{397}{10^6} = \frac{x}{4 \times 10^9}$$

We can cross-multiply and solve:

$$x = \frac{397}{10^6}(4 \times 10^9)$$

$$x = (397)(4 \times 10^3)$$

Hearing "approximately" and seeing the answer choices, we can take $397 \approx 400$.

$$x \approx (400)(4 \times 10^3)$$

$$= 16 \times 10^2 \times 10^3 = 16 \times 10^5 = 1{,}600{,}000$$

The correct answer is (C).

Luisa has c more children than Jenna has, and together they have a total of d children. Which of the following represents the number of children that Jenna has?

- $\frac{d-c}{2}$
- $d - \frac{c}{2}$
- $\frac{d}{2} - c$
- $2d - c$
- $d - 2c$

Jenna's Children

Luisa has c more children than Jenna has, and together they have a total of d children. Which of the following represents the number of children that Jenna has?

- $\frac{d-c}{2}$
- $d - \frac{c}{2}$
- $\frac{d}{2} - c$
- $2d - c$
- $d - 2c$

Explanation

Let's call the number of children of Luisa and Jenna L and J, respectively. Then we know that

$$L = J + c$$

$$L + J = d$$

We want to solve for J. We can substitute L into the second equation.

$$J + c + J = d$$

$$2J = d - c$$

$$J = \frac{d-c}{2}$$

The correct answer is (A).

If $10 + \frac{1}{y} = 20 - \frac{2}{y}$, then $y =$

- -1
- $\frac{1}{3}$
- $\frac{3}{10}$
- 2
- $\frac{1}{2}$

Linear Equation with Variable in Denominator

If $10 + \frac{1}{y} = 20 - \frac{2}{y}$, then $y =$

- -1
- $\frac{1}{3}$
- $\frac{3}{10}$
- 2
- $\frac{1}{2}$

Explanation

You can think of the equation in this question as $10 + x = 20 - 2x$, where x is an unknown we made up to stand for $\frac{1}{y}$. It's not an act of fancy math; on the contrary, it's looking at the equation and saying, "10 plus something is equal to 20 minus two times that something." So the difference between 10 and 20 is spanned by a total of three of the something's. So x must be $3\frac{1}{3} = \frac{10}{3}$; 10 and 20 are meeting partway between them by way of $3x$. In that case, y, the inverse of our x, is $\frac{3}{10}$. The textbook method here would be to multiply both sides of the equation by y and isolate the variable. The answer is (C).

Since that went a bit fast, we can expand on a more general point. When you face hard algebra or even easy algebra, you can sometimes make life easier for yourself by creating your own variable, working the problem and/or thinking in terms of that variable, and switching back at the end. For example, if you're faced with $x^4 + 6x^2 + 9$, you can introduce the variable $z = x^2$ and then solve the more familiar $z^2 + 6z + 9$ and then switch back to x after you have solved for z.

Again, the correct answer is (C).

During a certain season, a team won 80 percent of its first 80 games and 56 percent of its remaining games. If the team won $\frac{2}{3}$ of its games in the entire season, what was the total number of games that the team played?

- 180
- 170
- 156
- 120
- 105

Beginning and End of a Season

During a certain season, a team won 80 percent of its first 80 games and 56 percent of its remaining games. If the team won $\frac{2}{3}$ of its games in the entire season, what was the total number of games that the team played?

- 180
- 170
- 156
- 120
- 105

Explanation

This question is a good candidate for plugging in answer choices, but we can set up the equation first. Let's calculate the number of wins overall:

$$(0.80)80 + (0.56)R = \left(\frac{2}{3}\right)(80 + R),$$

Where R is the number of games remaining after the first 80. We are actually looking for $80 + R$. We can use the balance concept of averages here. The R games really pulled down the winning average, from 0.80 to approximately 0.67. Since that distance is about 0.13, and since the distance from 0.67 to 0.56 is 0.11, R must be greater than 80, probably about $\frac{13}{11}$ the size of 80. That rules out (C) through (E) and makes (A) appear probable. Let's try it. If $80 + R = 180$, then

$$(0.80)80 + (0.56)100 = \left(\frac{2}{3}\right)(180)$$

$$64 + 56 = 120$$

This statement is true. The correct answer is (A).

Of 41 reviews of a particular restaurant, 20 cited good service, 7 cited the quality of the desserts, and 20 cited neither good service nor the quality of the desserts. How many of the reviews cited good service and the quality of the desserts?

- 20
- 13
- 9
- 7
- 6

Restaurant Reviews – Overlapping Sets

Of 41 reviews of a particular restaurant, 20 cited good service, 7 cited the quality of the desserts, and 20 cited neither good service nor the quality of the desserts. How many of the reviews cited good service and the quality of the desserts?

- 20
- 13
- 9
- 7
- 6

Explanation

This is an overlapping sets question with two sets. We can optionally write the Venn diagram or we can simply recall the equation

$$T = G1 + G2 - B + N$$

Filling in what we know,

$$41 = 20 + 7 - B + 20$$

$$41 = 47 - B$$

So, $B = 6$.

The correct answer is (E).

What is the difference between the twelfth and eleventh terms of the sequence 0, 0, 1, 4, 9 … whose nth term is $2^{n-1} - n$?

- 20
- 31
- 63
- 123
- 1023

Terms in a Closed-Form Sequence

What is the difference between the twelfth and eleventh terms of the sequence 0, 0, 1, 4, 9 ... whose nth term is $2^{n-1} - n$?

- 20
- 31
- 63
- 123
- 1023

Explanation

The twelfth term of this sequence will have $n = 12$, so it will be $2^{12-1} - 12 = 2^{11} - 12$. Similarly, the 11th term will be $2^{11-1} - 11 = 2^{10} - 11$. Therefore, the difference between the two terms will be

$$2^{11} - 12 - (2^{10} - 11)$$

$$= 2^{11} - 2^{10} - 12 + 11$$

$$= 2^{11} - 2^{10} - 1$$

$$= 2^{10}(2^1 - 1) - 1$$

$$= 2^{10} - 1$$

If necessary, you can begin calculating to convince yourself that (D) is way too small. Or you may know that $2^{10} = 1024$ (or 1K, in computing terms, e.g., as in a file that takes up 1K of memory). Note that it was not necessary to compute previous terms to get the terms we wanted – the terms we wanted could be computed directly. In math terms, that means that this expression is a closed-form sequence, not a recursive sequence; GMAT questions may have one or the other.

The correct answer is (E).

If $(z-6)^2 = 625$, which of the following could be the value of $z + 6$?

- 31
- 19
- −13
- −19
- −31

Quadratic Equation

If $(z - 6)^2 = 625$, which of the following could be the value of $z + 6$?

- 31
- 19
- −13
- −19
- −31

Explanation

In this question, 625 is 25 squared. That is worth knowing, but if you didn't know that, you can see that the answer choices are all integers, so the square root of 625 is an integer. You could then see that the square is between 400 and 900, so the integer must be between 20 and 30, and it ends in 5, so the only possibility is 25. Having settled that, there are two cases: either we are dealing with a positive number or a negative number.

Case I: $z - 6 = 25$; $z = 31$; $z + 6 = 37$

Case II: $z - 6 = -25$; $z = -19$; $z + 6 = -13$

The correct answer is (C).

Ten percent of the members of a class are in the skiing club. Among the members of the class who are not in the skiing club, 40 have previously skied in their lives and 41 have never skied. How many members are there in the class?

- 90
- 100
- 120
- 144
- 162

Skiing Club Members...and the Whole Class

Ten percent of the members of a class are in the skiing club. Among the members of the class who are not in the skiing club, 40 have previously skied in their lives and 41 have never skied. How many members are there in the class?

- 90
- 100
- 120
- 144
- 162

Explanation

In this question we have a class and a club. We are told that 10% of the class is in the club, but then we get information about the rest of the class. Since among non-club members, 40 have skied and 41 have not, and since that's an either-or, we have a count of the 90% – it's 81. If 90% of the class is 81 people, then $\frac{9}{10}C = 81$ and the number of people in the class is

$$C = \frac{81}{\frac{9}{10}}$$

$$C = 81 \times \frac{10}{9} = 90$$

The correct answer is (A).

Nine audio recordings have an average (arithmetic mean) duration of 5.7 seconds and a median duration of 7.5 seconds. If the duration of the longest recording is 3.3 seconds more than twice the duration of the shortest recording, what is the maximum possible duration, in seconds, of the longest recording?

- 7.0
- 7.5
- 8.0
- 9.3
- 11.3

Nine Audio Recordings

Nine audio recordings have an average (arithmetic mean) duration of 5.7 seconds and a median duration of 7.5 seconds. If the duration of the longest recording is 3.3 seconds more than twice the duration of the shortest recording, what is the maximum possible duration, in seconds, of the longest recording?

- 7.0
- 7.5
- 8.0
- 9.3
- 11.3

Explanation

In this question, we have 9 recordings, with a recording of 7.5 seconds in the middle. Call the duration of the shortest recording x. Then, the question tells us, the longest is $2x + 3.3$. We want to find the largest possible maximum recording. In other words, there are different possible maximums, and we want to know the greatest of them. The average of 5.7 is known; to maximize the longest recording, we want to minimize the other ones, so that it has the most negative offset possible to have to net out and generate an average of 5.7. In the case in which everything else is minimal, not just the shortest, but all four recordings shorter than 7.5 seconds are x seconds long. Meanwhile, the recordings past the median have to be at least 7.5 seconds, but they could be only 7.5 seconds, so we'll make all three of them between the median and the longest 7.5 seconds. Then we can compute the sum of all the recordings

$$4x + 4(7.5) + 2x + 3.3 = 9(5.7)$$

The right side comes from the fact that sum of items = (average of items)(number of items).

$$6x + 4\left(\frac{15}{2}\right) + 3.3 = 9(5.7)$$

$$6x + 30 + 3.3 = 9(5.7)$$

$$6x + 30 + 3.3 = 45 + 6.3 = 51.3$$

$$6x = 51.3 - 33.3 = 18$$

$$x = 3$$

When $x = 3$, $2x + 3.3 = 9.3$.

The correct answer is (D).

In the results of a survey administered to the students in a particular class, $\frac{1}{3}$ identified themselves as citizens of the U.S. only, $\frac{1}{3}$ identified themselves as not U.S. citizens, $\frac{1}{10}$ identified themselves as citizens of both the U.S. and at least one other country, and 28 students did not reply to the survey. What is the number of students in the class?

- 60
- 110
- 120
- 200
- 400

Citizenship Survey

In the results of a survey administered to the students in a particular class, $\frac{1}{3}$ identified themselves as citizens of the U.S. only, $\frac{1}{3}$ identified themselves as not U.S. citizens, $\frac{1}{10}$ identified themselves as citizens of both the U.S. and at least one other country, and 28 students did not reply to the survey. What is the number of students in the class?

- 60
- 110
- 120
- 200
- 400

Explanation

If the number of people in the class are N, then

$$\frac{1}{3}N + \frac{1}{3}N + \frac{1}{10}N + 28 = N$$

Ballparking, we can see that $\frac{2}{3} + 10\% \approx 77\%$ of the class is everyone except about 23%, which is 28 people. Since 23 and 28 are close, one person is roughly one percent, and the total number will be close to 100, probably (B) or (C). And it can't be (B), because 110 is not divisible by 3 and so it would give non-integer numbers of people.

The correct answer is (C).

Four integers are randomly chosen from the set {−1, 0, 1}, with repetitions allowed. What is the probability that the product of the four integers chosen will be its least value possible?

- $\frac{1}{81}$
- $\frac{4}{81}$
- $\frac{8}{81}$
- $\frac{10}{81}$
- $\frac{16}{81}$

Probability of a Product

Four integers are randomly chosen from the set {−1, 0, 1}, with repetitions allowed. What is the probability that the product of the four integers chosen will be its least value possible?

- $\frac{1}{81}$
- $\frac{4}{81}$
- $\frac{8}{81}$
- $\frac{10}{81}$
- $\frac{16}{81}$

Explanation

There are only a couple possible products of these numbers. Indeed, we get a 0 if any of them are 0. We get a 1 if they are all 1's, and also if they are 1's and −1's such that the −1's are even in number. Finally, we can get a −1, the least possible, if we have an odd number of −1's and the rest of the factors 1's. So there are two ways to get a −1: with one −1 and three 1's. and with three −1's and one 1.

Let's start by finding the probability of getting one −1 and three 1's. There are four ways to do this: the negative one is first, second, third, or fourth. The probability of any one specific draw is $\frac{1}{3} \times \frac{1}{3} \times \frac{1}{3} \times \frac{1}{3} = \frac{1}{81}$. Since there are four independent probabilities, we add them to get the odds of obtaining any one of them, so the odds are $\frac{4}{81}$ of one −1 and three 1's. The logic is identical to draw one positive 1 and three negative 1's, so that case also obtains with probability $\frac{4}{81}$. The probability of obtaining one or the other of these two exclusive cases is their sum (in probability "or" usually means "add"): so $\frac{8}{81}$ are the odds that our product will be −1, the least possible value.

The correct answer is (C).

$$1.001 + \frac{0.999996}{1.002} =$$

- 1.993
- 1.998
- 1.999
- 1.9999
- 2

Suggestive Fraction

$$1.001 + \frac{0.999996}{1.002} =$$

- 1.993
- 1.998
- 1.999
- 1.9999
- 2

Explanation

In this question, the given expression looks like about 2, but the answer choices are all about 2, so we're not going to be able to estimate the correct answer. We can try to break up the numbers into logically distinct pieces. Each of them is 1 plus or minus a small number, so we can break them apart in that fashion:

$$1.001 + \frac{0.999996}{1.002}$$

$$= 1 + 10^{-3} + \frac{1 - 4(10^{-6})}{1 + 2(10^{-3})}$$

Something is going on between the numerator and the denominator of the fraction. Is the top the square of the bottom? No, but it is a difference of squares, since it's of the form $a^2 - b^2$, and hence it can be factored as $(a-b)(a+b)$:

$$= 1 + 10^{-3} + \frac{[1 + 2(10^{-3})][1 - 2(10^{-3})]}{1 + 2(10^{-3})}$$

The $1 + 2(10^{-3})$ in numerator and denominator cancel:

$$= 1 + 10^{-3} + 1 - 2(10^{-3})$$

$$= 2 - 10^{-3}$$

$$= 2 - 0.001 = 1.999$$

The correct answer is (C).

If 60 percent of a class answered the first question on a certain test correctly, 60 percent answered the second question on the test correctly, and 60 percent answered both questions correctly, what percent answered neither question correctly?

- 0%
- 20%
- 30%
- 40%
- 60%

Overlapping Sets – Questions Answered Correctly

If 60 percent of a class answered the first question on a certain test correctly, 60 percent answered the second question on the test correctly, and 60 percent answered both questions correctly, what percent answered neither question correctly?

- 0%
- 20%
- 30%
- 40%
- 60%

Explanation

We can think of this as an overlapping sets question, drawing a Venn diagram or simply recalling the formula $T = G1 + G2 - B + N$. If we call the total number of students 100, then we have

$$100 = 60 + 60 - 60 + N$$

$$100 = 60 + N$$

$$N = 40$$

The correct answer is (D).

The probability is $\frac{1}{2}$ that a certain coin will yield heads on any given toss. If the coin is tossed five times, what is the probability that at least one of the tosses will yield heads?

- $\frac{1}{2}$
- $\frac{3}{4}$
- $\frac{7}{8}$
- $\frac{31}{32}$
- $\frac{63}{64}$

Probability of Coin Tosses

The probability is $\frac{1}{2}$ that a certain coin will yield heads on any given toss. If the coin is tossed five times, what is the probability that at least one of the tosses will yield heads?

- $\frac{1}{2}$
- $\frac{3}{4}$
- $\frac{7}{8}$
- $\frac{31}{32}$
- $\frac{63}{64}$

Explanation

This question asks for the probability that at least one of five tosses is heads. There are a lot of ways for that to happen, but only one way for it *not* to happen, which is that all five tosses are tails. So we'll find the probability of that. We want the probability of five tails in a row. That will be $\left(\frac{1}{2}\right)^5$. We multiply, not add, because we are calculating the probability of a chain of events, not that we get one of a bunch of options. Another way to look at it is that we are talking about getting a tails *and* another tails and so on, and "and" usually means multiplication in probability. Anyway, $\left(\frac{1}{2}\right)^5 = \frac{1}{2^5} = \frac{1}{32}$. That's all tails. So the odds that anything except that happens are $1 - \frac{1}{32} = \frac{31}{32}$.

The correct answer is (D).

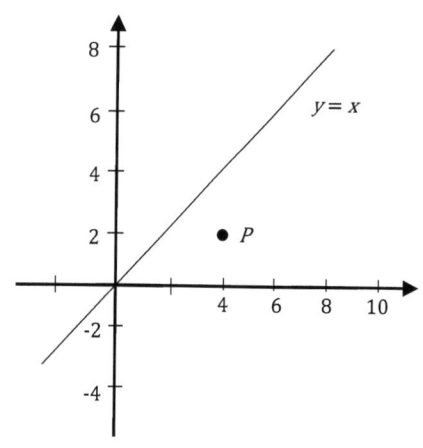

In the rectangular coordinate system above, point Q (not shown) is the same distance from the line y = x as point P, and it is the same distance from the y axis as point P is from the x axis. Point R (not shown) lies at both the same distance from the x axis and the same distance from the y axis as point Q, but is in a different location. If the coordinates of point P are (4,2), which of the following are possible coordinates of point R?

- (−4,−2)
- (−4,5)
- (2,−4)
- (4,−2)
- (−4,−5)

Distances in the Coordinate Plane

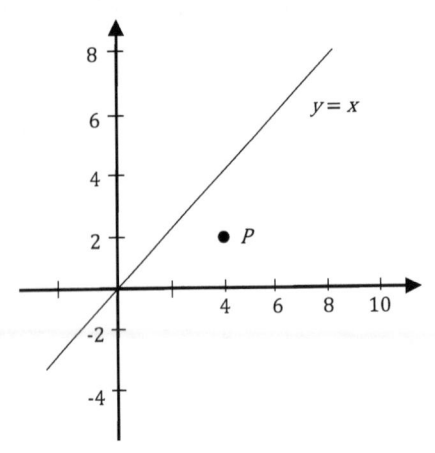

In the rectangular coordinate system above, point Q (not shown) is the same distance from the line $y = x$ as point P, and it is the same distance from the y axis as point P is from the x axis. Point R (not shown) lies at both the same distance from the x axis and the same distance from the y axis as point Q, but is in a different location. If the coordinates of point P are (4,2), which of the following are possible coordinates of point R?

- (−4,−2)
- (−4,5)
- (2,−4)
- (4,−2)
- (−4,−5)

Explanation

In this question, point P resides at the coordinates (4, 2). The not-shown point Q is "the same distance from the y axis as point P is from the x axis." That little phrase means that since point P has a y coordinate of 2, point Q will have an x coordinate of 2, and will thus be (2, ?). It will therefore have coordinates (2, 4), since it is equidistant from $y = x$. Finally, since point R is the same distance from each axis as point Q, it must have an x coordinate of ±2 and a y coordinate of ±4.

The correct answer is (C).

If $y < 0$, which of the following must decrease as y decreases?

I. $10y - 100$

II. $\frac{y-1}{y}$

III. $y^2 - y$

- I only
- III only
- I and II
- I and III
- II and III

Decreasing with Y

If $y < 0$, which of the following must decrease as y decreases?

I. $10y - 100$

II. $\frac{y-1}{y}$

III. $y^2 - y$

- o   I only
- o   III only
- o   I and II
- o   I and III
- o   II and III

Explanation

In this question, y is negative, and we are imagining the situation in which it's traveling to the left down the number line. Roman numeral I definitely also travels down the number line – even faster than y does, in fact.

For II, we can reformat as $1 - \frac{1}{y}$. Since fractions are involved, we can try fractional y's. I'm trying to disprove this by finding increase. Say y goes from $-\frac{1}{100}$ to -10. That's a decrease in y. The expression goes from $1 + 100 = 101$ to $1 + \frac{1}{10}$, so it decreased as well. You can break it down into the case in which the absolute value of y is less than one, greater than one, or crosses. We just did crossing. Meanwhile, if y goes from -10 to -100, this thing goes from $\frac{11}{10}$ or $\frac{110}{100}$ to $\frac{101}{100}$. If y goes from $-\frac{1}{4}$ to $-\frac{1}{2}$, the expression goes from 5 to 4. At this point, we should stop and conclude that it decreases, but see the note below.

On to III. This thing need not decrease. For example, when y goes from -1 to -10, this thing moves from 2 to 110. I is in, and III is out. The correct answer is (C), I and II.

The ideal situation when evaluating by cases is that you can extrapolate a rule from the cases after a couple. In Roman numeral II here, it boils down to the properties of what we could call $x = 1 - \frac{1}{y}$. In the coordinate plane, this is a hyperbola – something that does not appear in the official test rubric, but which indirectly appears in some questions. You can play around with such equations on a graphing calculator (if you know someone in high school) or on a site such as Wolfram Alpha. Nevertheless, sometimes when evaluating by cases, it is difficult to know whether we have been exhaustive, and therefore whether we have been conclusive. It is critical not to get stuck in this cases. Make an evaluation and move on, even if it's not totally conclusive.

Again, the correct answer is (C).

A school currently maintains a fixed number of students per class. If the ratio of students per class were to be increased by 1, 10 fewer classes would be run for a total of 120 students. What is the current ratio of students per class?

- 3
- 4
- 6
- 8
- 12

STUDENTS PER CLASS

A school currently maintains a fixed number of students per class. If the ratio of students per class were to be increased by 1, 10 fewer classes would be run for a total of 120 students. What is the current ratio of students per class?

- 3
- 4
- 6
- 8
- 12

EXPLANATION

In some questions we have a constant ratio that we work with. In this case, the ratio changes, and the number of classes changes, but the total number of students stays the same. Focusing on the units, we can write

$$\frac{\text{students}}{\text{class}} (\text{number of classes}) = 120$$

On the left, both the ratio and the number of classes are integers, since we are not dealing with fractional students or classes. So, looking at the answer choices, we could be talking about 3 students per class and 40 classes, 4 students per class and 30 classes, and so on. Actually, there we have our answer: if we increase the students per class from 3 to 4, the number of classes decreases from 40 to 30, just as the question indicates. So the current ratio is 3.

The correct answer is (A).

A rectangular box is 5 inches wide, 5 inches long, and 10 inches high. If *x* is the greatest possible (straight-line) distance, in inches, between any two points on the box, and *y* is the second-greatest such distance, what is the ratio of *x* to *y*?

- $\sqrt{\dfrac{6}{5}}$

- $\dfrac{6}{5}$

- $\dfrac{\sqrt{6}}{2}$

- $\sqrt{3}$

- 2

Distance within a Box

A rectangular box is 5 inches wide, 5 inches long, and 10 inches high. If x is the greatest possible (straight-line) distance, in inches, between any two points on the box, and y is the second-greatest such distance, what is the ratio of x to y?

- $\sqrt{\dfrac{6}{5}}$

- $\dfrac{6}{5}$

- $\dfrac{\sqrt{6}}{2}$

- $\sqrt{3}$

- 2

Explanation

It's usually a good idea to make a quick sketch on geometry questions:

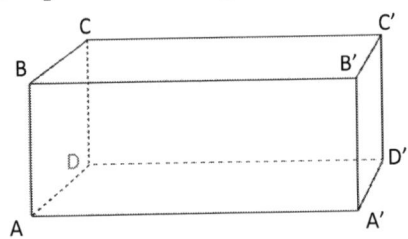

The lengths of all of the edges of this shape are either 5 or 10. The lines joining points AA', DD', and so on, are all 10. The length AD' is the hypotenuse of a triangle with sides 5 and 10, so its length is

$$AD' = \sqrt{5^2 + 10^2} = \sqrt{125},$$

by the Pythagorean Theorem. However, AD' is not the longest segment connecting two points. Namely, AC' is longer because it is the hypotenuse of a triangle that has AD' as a base, so its length is

$$AC' = \sqrt{5^2 + \left(\sqrt{125}\right)^2}$$

$$= \sqrt{25 + 125} = \sqrt{150}$$

These are the two-longest lines connecting two points on the box, so the sought-after ratio is

$$\frac{\sqrt{150}}{\sqrt{125}} = \sqrt{\frac{150}{125}} = \sqrt{\frac{6}{5}}.$$

The correct answer is (A).

A dollar amount of 5x was distributed evenly among three charitable organizations, A, B, and C. However, after it was determined that Organization C was ineligible for its share, its share was given to Organization B. Organization B chose to give Organization A the portion of Organization C's share that Organization A would have received if Organization C's share had been evenly split among four organizations including Organization A. What was the dollar amount, in terms of x, that Organization A ultimately obtained?

- $\dfrac{5x}{4}$
- $\dfrac{17x}{12}$
- $\dfrac{5x}{3}$
- $\dfrac{23x}{12}$
- $\dfrac{25x}{12}$

Distribution of Charitable Donation

A dollar amount of 5x was distributed evenly among three charitable organizations, A, B, and C. However, after it was determined that Organization C was ineligible for its share, its share was given to Organization B. Organization B chose to give Organization A the portion of Organization C's share that Organization A would have received if Organization C's share had been evenly split among four organizations including Organization A. What was the dollar amount, in terms of x, that Organization A ultimately obtained?

- $\dfrac{5x}{4}$
- $\dfrac{17x}{12}$
- $\dfrac{5x}{3}$
- $\dfrac{23x}{12}$
- $\dfrac{25x}{12}$

Explanation

This question rambles a bit, so right off the bat we can pick a case to understand what is being said. Let's say that $5x = 60$ and we are talking about $60 here. While 100 is nice for calculating percentages, here we are doing dividing and 60 is highly divisible. The plan is that A, B, and C each get $20, but C gives its $20 to B. B then chooses to give a fourth of the $20 to A, so B gives A $5. Therefore, A gets a total of $25. We may have sufficient information now to determine the answer; we can see which one or ones yield 25 when we set $x = 12$. Choice (A) gives 15, (B) gives 17, (C) gives 20, (D) gives 23, and (E) gives 25. Choices (A) through (D) are therefore out.

The correct answer is (E).

The average (arithmetic mean) of a set of n numbers is 75. If adding the number 160 in the set raises the average to 80, what is the value of n?

- 20
- 16
- 8
- 6
- 4

Average with New Element

The average (arithmetic mean) of a set of n numbers is 75. If adding the number 160 in the set raises the average to 80, what is the value of n?

- 20
- 16
- 8
- 6
- 4

Explanation

In this question, since sum of items = (average of items)(number of items), the initial set of n numbers sums to $75n$. Therefore, when we add the number 160, we have a new total of $75n + 160$, and $n + 1$ numbers, so the average is

$$\frac{75n + 160}{n + 1} = 80$$

$$75n + 160 = 80n + 80$$

$$80 = 5n$$

$$16 = n$$

The correct answer is (B).

The ratio, by volume, of salt to sugar to water in a certain solution is 3:5:7. The solution will be altered so the ratio of sugar to salt is doubled while the ratio of sugar to water is maintained. If altered solution will contain 7 cubic centimeters of water, how many cubic centimeters of salt will it contain?

- 1.5
- 3
- 5
- 10
- 14

Ratio of Substances in a Solution

The ratio, by volume, of salt to sugar to water in a certain solution is 3:5:7. The solution will be altered so the ratio of sugar to salt is doubled while the ratio of sugar to water is maintained. If altered solution will contain 7 cubic centimeters of water, how many cubic centimeters of salt will it contain?

- 1.5
- 3
- 5
- 10
- 14

Explanation

In this question, we have a three-part ratio, so we can keep track of it with the colon notation or a table:

Salt	Sugar	Water
3	5	7
3	10	14

The second row is the desired ratio. First we put in a 10 to double the ratio of sugar to salt. Then, to keep the ratio of sugar to water the same, we have to double the water also. Then we learn that the actual value of water is 7, or half the entry in the row, so the actual value for salt will be half its entry, or 1.5.

The correct answer is (A).

If $n = 3 \times 4 \times p$, where p is a prime number greater than 3, how many different positive non-prime divisors does n have, excluding 1 and n?

- Six
- Seven
- Eight
- Nine
- Ten

Non-Prime Divisors of N

If $n = 3 \times 4 \times p$, where p is a prime number greater than 3, how many different positive non-prime divisors does n have, excluding 1 and n?

- Six
- Seven
- Eight
- Nine
- Ten

Explanation

In this question, we are given n in a form that is almost its prime factorization, which is $n = 2^2 \times 3 \times p$. To determine the number of divisors sought, we essentially have to count different combinations of the factors. We can break down the possibilities by the number of prime factors used to form each divisor. We can't have any divisors of just one prime factor, because the question stipulates that we count "non-prime" divisors. In the case that our divisor has two factors, it could be (2)(2), or (2)(3), or (2)(p), or (3)(p), for a total of 4 possibilities. In the case that our divisor has three prime factors, it could be (2)(2)(3), or (2)(3)(p), or (2)(2)(p), for a total of 3 possibilities. The case that our divisor has four prime factors is out, because that equals n, and we have been told to exclude n. Therefore, we have 7 possibilities of the type described.

The correct answer is (B).

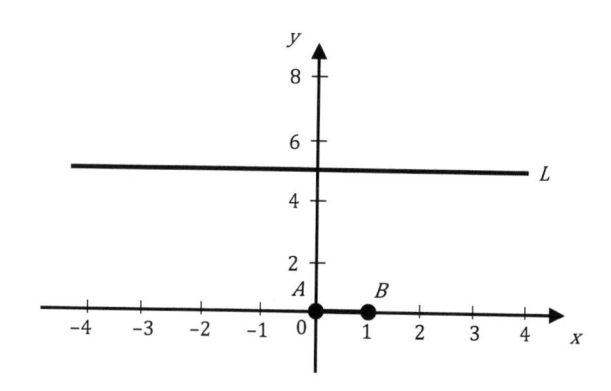

In the rectangular coordinate system above, if a point C along line L is chosen to form a triangle with the segment AB, what is the area of triangle ABC?

- 1
- 2.5
- 5
- 10
- The area cannot be determined from the given information.

Triangle in the Coordinate Plane

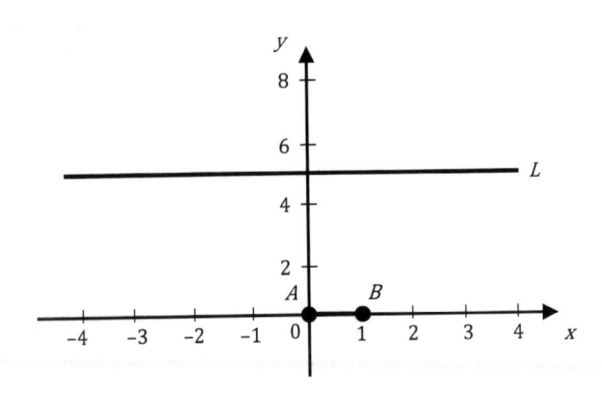

In the rectangular coordinate system above, if a point C along line L is chosen to form a triangle with the segment AB, what is the area of triangle ABC?

- 1
- 2.5
- 5
- 10
- The area cannot be determined from the given information.

Explanation

This question gives us a rule for how the triangle ABC can be constructed and it asks us to determine the area of the triangle, if we can. To find the area of a triangle, we need a valid base-height pair. We can take AB as the base and imagine a particular triangle ABC. The definition of the height relative to AB is that it's the length of the line that is perpendicular to the base and which joins the other vertex of the triangle with the base, or an extension of the base. That means that the height of the triangle is 5 not only when point C is between A and B – it's always 5, in fact. Therefore, $\frac{1}{2}bh = \frac{1}{2}(1)(5) = 2.5$.

The correct answer is (B).

Car A and Car B are driving toward each other along a straight line. Car A travels at a constant speed of 60 miles per hour and Car B travels at a constant speed of 40 miles per hour. If at noon they are separated by a distance of 300 miles, at what time will they meet?

- 2:40 pm
- 3:00 pm
- 3:20 pm
- 3:40 pm
- 4:00 pm

Approaching Cars

Car A and Car B are driving toward each other along a straight line. Car A travels at a constant speed of 60 miles per hour and Car B travels at a constant speed of 40 miles per hour. If at noon they are separated by a distance of 300 miles, at what time will they meet?

- 2:40 pm
- 3:00 pm
- 3:20 pm
- 3:40 pm
- 4:00 pm

Explanation

This question is more of a combined rate question than a speed question. We care only indirectly about the individual speeds of the cars and directly about how quickly the gap between the cars closes. In fact, the distance between the cars is closing at a rate of 60 + 40 = 100 miles per hour. Since the distance is initially 300 miles, it will therefore take three hours to close the gap. They begin at noon, so they meet at three o'clock. The correct answer is (B).

As you can see, the combined rate approach to this question is incredibly swift. You could solve the question by constructing three equations with the speed formula, but it's fairly laborious. To be sure to take advantage of the opportunity to use combined rates whenever it's at hand, take note whenever a question has more than one rate. If there's more than one speed or other rate, those multiple rates possibly can be added or subtracted.

Again, the correct answer is (B).

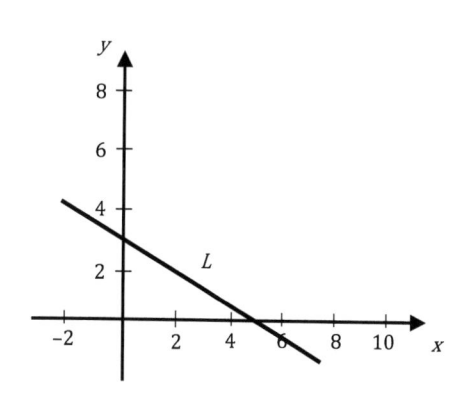

In the coordinate system above, which of the following is the equation of line L?

- $3x - 5y = 15$
- $3x + 5y = 15$
- $5x + 3y = 15$
- $3x - 5y = -15$
- $5x - 3y = 15$

Equation of Line L

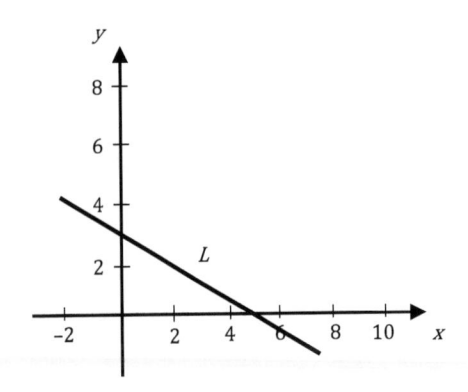

In the coordinate system above, which of the following is the equation of line L?

- $3x - 5y = 15$
- $3x + 5y = 15$
- $5x + 3y = 15$
- $3x - 5y = -15$
- $5x - 3y = 15$

Explanation

In this question, the line crosses the axes at (0, 3) and (5, 0). Therefore, both of those cases should work in the correct answer choice. We can try (0, 3) first by plugging $x = 0, y = 3$ into the answer choices. Choice (B) works and (D) works, but the other equations yield falsehoods. Testing the second case on (B) and (D), $x = 5, y = 0$, only (B) works.

The correct answer is (B).

$$\left(\frac{x+1}{x-1}\right)^2$$

If $x > 1$, and if $x = \frac{1}{y}$, then the expression above is equivalent to

- $\left(\frac{y+1}{y-1}\right)^2$
- $\left(\frac{y-1}{y+1}\right)^2$
- $\frac{y^2+1}{1-y^2}$
- $\frac{y^2-1}{y^2+1}$
- $-\left(\frac{y-1}{y+1}\right)^2$

Substitution Into an Expression

$$\left(\frac{x+1}{x-1}\right)^2$$

If $x > 1$, and if $x = \frac{1}{y}$, then the expression above is equivalent to

- $\left(\frac{y+1}{y-1}\right)^2$
- $\left(\frac{y-1}{y+1}\right)^2$
- $\frac{y^2+1}{1-y^2}$
- $\frac{y^2-1}{y^2+1}$
- $-\left(\frac{y-1}{y+1}\right)^2$

Explanation

This question could be solved the old-fashioned way by plugging in $\frac{1}{y}$ for x in the original expression and simplify it, primarily by multiplying it by versions of 1. That will be fairly work-intensive, however. We can try picking a specific case and seeing which answer choices match it.

Say $x = 2$. In that case,

$$\left(\frac{x+1}{x-1}\right)^2 = \left(\frac{3}{1}\right)^2 = 9,$$

and $y = \frac{1}{x} = \frac{1}{2}$. We can therefore plug $\frac{1}{2}$ in for y in the answer choices and see which of them generate 9. Any that do not can't be the correct answer. (A) yields

$$\left(\frac{\frac{1}{2}+1}{\frac{1}{2}-1}\right)^2 = \left(\frac{\frac{3}{2}}{-\frac{1}{2}}\right)^2 = (-3)^2 = 9,$$

So it could be correct. (B) is the inverse, so it will give $\frac{1}{9}$ and it's out. (C) gives $\frac{5}{4}$ over $\frac{3}{4}$, which is not 9. (D) and (E) are both negative, so they are not 9.

The correct answer is (A).

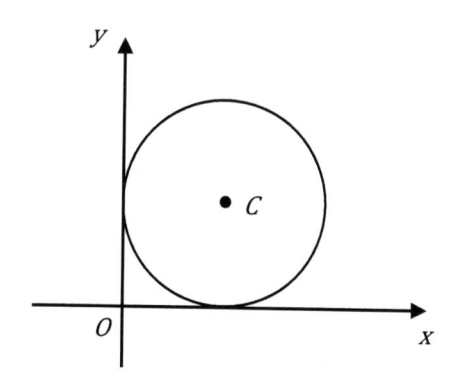

The circle with center C shown above is tangent to both axes and has an area of A. What is the distance from O to C, in terms of A?

- A
- $\sqrt{\dfrac{2A}{\pi}}$
- $\sqrt{\dfrac{3A}{\pi}}$
- $\dfrac{2A}{\pi}$
- $\dfrac{3A}{\pi}$

Tangent Circle

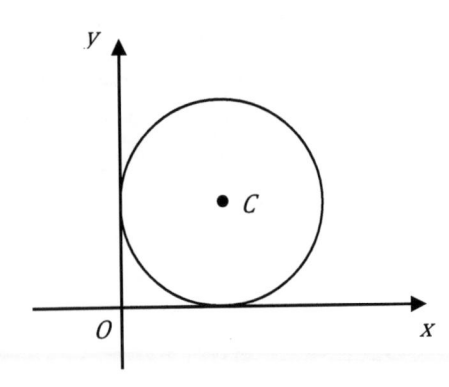

The circle with center C shown above is tangent to both axes and has an area of A. What is the distance from O to C, in terms of A?

- A
- $\sqrt{\dfrac{2A}{\pi}}$
- $\sqrt{\dfrac{3A}{\pi}}$
- $\dfrac{2A}{\pi}$
- $\dfrac{3A}{\pi}$

Explanation

In this question, we can find the radius r in terms of A by manipulating the area formula, $A = \pi r^2$:

$$r^2 = \dfrac{A}{\pi}$$

$$r = \sqrt{\dfrac{A}{\pi}}$$

Point C in the figure is the upper-right point of a square that has sides of length r. And the distance from the origin to C is the diagonal of the square, so it is the hypotenuse of a right triangle with height r and base r, so the distance will equal

$$\sqrt{r^2 + r^2} = \sqrt{\dfrac{A}{\pi} + \dfrac{A}{\pi}} = \sqrt{\dfrac{2A}{\pi}}$$

The correct answer is (B).

A game is played with a six-sided, regularly numbered die. The player starts with a number equal to 0.1n, where n is an integer between 1 and 6, inclusive. On each of 20 subsequent rolls, if the number rolled times 0.1 is greater than or equal to the player's current number, the player's current number is incremented by 0.1; if the number rolled times 0.1 is less than the player's current number and is odd, the player's number is decremented by 0.1; if the number rolled times 0.1 is less than the player's current number and is even, the player's number is unaffected. If 55% of the die rolls in a particular game are even, which of the following is a possible final value of that game?

I. 0.8

II. 0.5

III. 0.1

- I only
- I and II only
- I and III only
- II and III only
- I, II, and III

Game with Six-Sided Die

A game is played with a six-sided, regularly numbered die. The player starts with a number equal to $0.1n$, where n is an integer between 1 and 6, inclusive. On each of 20 subsequent rolls, if the number rolled times 0.1 is greater than or equal to the player's current number, the player's current number is incremented by 0.1; if the number rolled times 0.1 is less than the player's current number and is odd, the player's number is decremented by 0.1; if the number rolled times 0.1 is less than the player's current number and is even, the player's number is unaffected. If 55% of the die rolls in a particular game are even, which of the following is a possible final value of that game?

I. 0.8

II. 0.5

III. 0.1

- I only
- I and II only
- I and III only
- II and III only
- I, II, and III

Explanation

In this question, we are described a game that has a lot of instructions and doesn't seem very entertaining. The question poses the case that we roll 20 times and 55% of the rolls are positive, which means 11 of the 20 rolls are positive. We can imagine some cases: what happens if we roll 6 eleven times and 5 nine times? I'm looking for a maximum score here. If the player's score is 0.6 and he rolls a six, the score goes up to 0.7, but there's no case in which the score can advance further; it can either stay or go down. So Roman numeral I, a final score of 0.8, is impossible. That leaves only answer choice (D). There was a bit of luck here, but when analyzing by cases, extreme cases tend to be easier to test and tend to give insight into the situation. If we had to explore further we could have evaluated the game's minimum score.

The correct answer is (D).

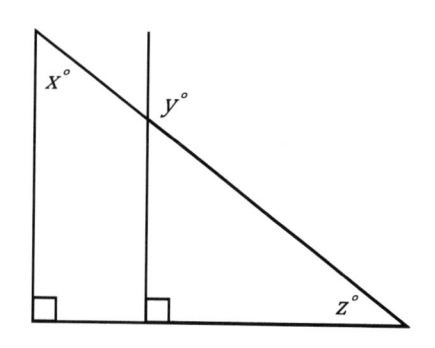

In the figure above, if $x = 40$, then $y - z =$

- 60
- 70
- 80
- 90
- 100

Interior and Exterior Angles of Triangle

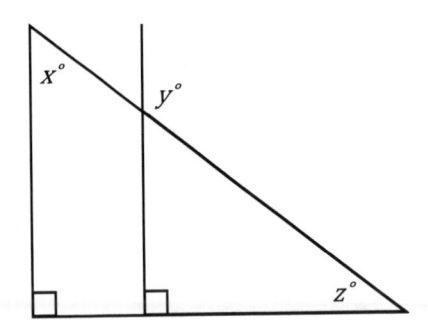

In the figure above, if $x = 40$, then $y - z =$

- 60
- 70
- 80
- 90
- 100

Explanation

In this question, the fact that the two vertical lines are both perpendicular to a common line means they are parallel to each other. That means that the angle just "under" y is equal to x, and since it is supplementary to that angle, and that angle is 40, $y = 180 - 40 = 140$. Moreover, since z is the third angle in a triangle with angles of 90 and 40 degrees, $z = 180 - 90 - 40 = 50$. Therefore, $y - z = 140 - 50 = 90$.

The correct answer is (D).

If $\frac{1}{c} - \frac{1}{c+3} = \frac{1}{c+5}$, then c could be

- $\sqrt{15}$
- 1
- 0
- −1
- −7

Non-Linear Equation

If $\frac{1}{c} - \frac{1}{c+3} = \frac{1}{c+5}$, then c could be

- ○ $\sqrt{15}$
- ○ 1
- ○ 0
- ○ −1
- ○ −7

Explanation

In this question, finding a common denominator or multiplying across would get a bit ugly, so we can try cases from the answer choices. We'll skip (A) for now. We can try (B), where $c = 1$. That gives $1 - \frac{1}{4} = \frac{1}{6}$, which is false, so (B) is out. (C) is out, because we cannot have $\frac{1}{0}$. In (D), $-1 - \frac{1}{2} = \frac{1}{4}$ is false. In (E), $-\frac{1}{7} - \frac{1}{-4} = \frac{1}{-2}$ or $-\frac{1}{7} + \frac{1}{4} = -\frac{1}{2}$ is false. We have eliminated everything except (A).

The correct answer is (A).

If two two-digit positive integers have their tens digits exchanged, the difference between the resulting pair of integers differs from the difference between the original pair of numbers by 4. What is the greatest possible difference between the original pair of integers?

- 76
- 80
- 82
- 90
- 94

Exchanging Digits

If two two-digit positive integers have their tens digits exchanged, the difference between the resulting pair of integers differs from the difference between the original pair of numbers by 4. What is the greatest possible difference between the original pair of integers?

- 76
- 80
- 82
- 90
- 94

Explanation

This question could be described through algebra, but it's well suited for analysis by cases. Let's try a case with two two-digit numbers, 17 and 21. If their tens digits are switched, we get 27 and 11. The difference between the first pair is 4 and the difference between the second pair is 16, so the difference has changed by $16 - 4 = 12 \neq 4$ and hence this case is invalid. We can try 17 and 25, which differ by 8. When we flip, they are 27 and 15, which differ by 12. The difference has changed by $12 - 8 = 4$, so this is a valid pair of numbers.

Now that we understand the rule, we want to find the biggest possible original difference, which will be between 76 and 90, per the answer choices. Keeping the units digits from our previous case, how about 97 and 15? They differ by 82. When we flip, they are 17 and 95, and they differ by 78. The difference has changed by $82 - 78 = 4$, so this is a valid case. The original difference was 82, so we can conclude that (C) could be the answer and that (A) and (B) are definitely out. We can try to construct an initial difference of 90 or 94. These cases are impossible, because the smallest two-digit number, 10, would push the other number to 100 or above, and it would no longer be a two-digit number.

The correct answer is (C).

At a large company, the probabilities of success of three distinct new product launches are independently $\frac{1}{4}$, $\frac{1}{2}$, and $\frac{5}{8}$, respectively. What is the probability that exactly two of the launches succeed?

- $\frac{7}{8}$
- $\frac{1}{2}$
- $\frac{23}{64}$
- $\frac{5}{64}$
- $\frac{3}{64}$

Three Product Launches

At a large company, the probabilities of success of three distinct new product launches are independently $\frac{1}{4}$, $\frac{1}{2}$, and $\frac{5}{8}$, respectively. What is the probability that exactly two of the launches succeed?

- $\frac{7}{8}$
- $\frac{1}{2}$
- $\frac{23}{64}$
- $\frac{5}{64}$
- $\frac{3}{64}$

Explanation

In this question, if we call these launches A, B, and C, there are three possible ways that exactly two of the launches succeed. Case I: A fails, B and C succeed. Case II: B fails, A and C succeed. Case III: C fails, A and B succeed. We can compute the probability of each case, and then add them for the probability of the described result.

Case I: $\frac{3}{4} \times \frac{1}{2} \times \frac{5}{8} = \frac{15}{64}$

Case II: $\frac{1}{4} \times \frac{1}{2} \times \frac{5}{8} = \frac{5}{64}$

Case III: $\frac{1}{4} \times \frac{1}{2} \times \frac{3}{8} = \frac{3}{64}$

The overall probability is thus $\frac{23}{64}$.

The correct answer is (C).

If $\frac{1}{1+\frac{1}{x}} = 2$, then $x =$

- -2
- -1
- 0
- 1
- 2

Solving for x in Compound Fraction

If $\dfrac{1}{1+\frac{1}{x}} = 2$, then $x =$

- ○ −2
- ○ −1
- ○ 0
- ○ 1
- ○ 2

Explanation

The algebra in this question is not bad. We can cross multiply the equation to get

$$\dfrac{1}{1+\dfrac{1}{x}} = 2$$

$$2 + \dfrac{2}{x} = 1$$

And multiply through by x:

$$2x + 2 = x$$

$$x = -2$$

The correct answer is (A).

How quickly heat transfers through an insulating layer depends on that insulator's thermal resistance. If two insulators are used together, the inverse of the combined thermal resistance is sum of the reciprocals of each layer's thermal resistance. If the thermal resistances of two insulators are r and $2r$, what is their combined resistance?

- $2r^2$
- $3r$
- $\dfrac{1}{3r}$
- $\dfrac{2r}{3}$
- $\dfrac{3}{2r}$

Thermal Resistances

How quickly heat transfers through an insulating layer depends on that insulator's thermal resistance. If two insulators are used together, the inverse of the combined thermal resistance is sum of the reciprocals of each layer's thermal resistance. If the thermal resistances of two insulators are r and $2r$, what is their combined resistance?

- $2r^2$
- $3r$
- $\dfrac{1}{3r}$
- $\dfrac{2r}{3}$
- $\dfrac{3}{2r}$

Explanation

In this question, while the subject matter is different, the math described is similar to what we do in a combined rate question when we are given times: we add reciprocals to get a combined effect. Based on the question we can write

$$\frac{1}{r} + \frac{1}{2r} = \frac{1}{C},$$

where we are looking for C. If you know the $\frac{AB}{A+B}$ formula from combined work, you can plug in r and $2r$ and you'll have your answer. Otherwise, we can get a common denominator:

$$\frac{2}{2r} + \frac{1}{2r} = \frac{1}{C}$$

$$\frac{3}{2r} = \frac{1}{C}$$

$$3C = 2r$$

$$C = \frac{2r}{3}$$

The correct answer is (D).

A particular class was given a quiz consisting of two questions, which were marked either correct or incorrect. Of the 150 students, 100 got the first question correct and 120 got the second question correct. If at least 10 students got neither question correct, then the number of students who got both questions correct could be any number from

- 10 to 30
- 20 to 50
- 30 to 100
- 80 to 100
- 80 to 120

Students Who Got Both Questions Correct

A particular class was given a quiz consisting of two questions, which were marked either correct or incorrect. Of the 150 students, 100 got the first question correct and 120 got the second question correct. If at least 10 students got neither question correct, then the number of students who got both questions correct could be any number from

- 10 to 30
- 20 to 50
- 30 to 100
- 80 to 100
- 80 to 120

Explanation

This is an overlapping sets question of two sets, so we can draw a Venn diagram or cut straight to the formula $T = G1 + G2 - B + N$. Filling in what we know, we get

$$150 = 100 + 120 - B + N$$

We care about B, so we can isolate it:

$$150 = 220 - B + N$$

$$B = 70 + N$$

The question tells us that N must be at least 10, so B must be at least 80. That narrows the answer choices to (D) and (E). From an arithmetic standpoint, B could range freely; the upper constraint is logically derived. It boils down to the fact that if 100 got the first question correct, then the number that got both questions correct cannot be greater than 100.

The correct answer is (D).

$\left(\frac{1}{3}\right)^{-3} \left(\frac{1}{9}\right)^{-2} \left(\frac{1}{27}\right)^{-1} \left(\frac{1}{81}\right)^{0} =$

- $\left(\frac{1}{3}\right)^{-36}$
- $\left(\frac{1}{3}\right)^{-10}$
- $\left(\frac{1}{3}\right)^{-11}$
- $\left(\frac{1}{9}\right)^{-10}$
- $\left(\frac{1}{9}\right)^{-11}$

Differing Powers and Denominators

$$\left(\frac{1}{3}\right)^{-3} \left(\frac{1}{9}\right)^{-2} \left(\frac{1}{27}\right)^{-1} \left(\frac{1}{81}\right)^{0} =$$

- $\left(\frac{1}{3}\right)^{-36}$
- $\left(\frac{1}{3}\right)^{-10}$
- $\left(\frac{1}{3}\right)^{-11}$
- $\left(\frac{1}{9}\right)^{-10}$
- $\left(\frac{1}{9}\right)^{-11}$

Explanation

In this question, we can make this expression simple by converting all of the exponents into the same base, 3:

$$(3^{-1})^{-3}(3^{-2})^{-2}(3^{-3})^{-1}(3^{-4})^{0}$$

Exponents taken to exponents multiply, so this gives us

$$3^3 3^4 3^3 3^0 = 3^{3+4+3+0} = 3^{10}$$

This is the same as answer choice (B), which is $(3^{-1})^{-10} = 3^{10}$.

The correct answer is (B).

Mixture A of spices is 60 percent parsley and 40 percent oregano by weight. Mixture B of spices is 25 percent parsley and 75 percent thyme. If a mixture of A and B contains 35 percent parsley, approximately what percent of the weight of the mixture is A?

- 28%
- $33\frac{1}{3}\%$
- 40%
- $66\frac{2}{3}\%$
- 72%

Mixture of Spices

Mixture A of spices is 60 percent parsley and 40 percent oregano by weight. Mixture B of spices is 25 percent parsley and 75 percent thyme. If a mixture of A and B contains 35 percent parsley, approximately what percent of the weight of the mixture is A?

- 28%
- $33\frac{1}{3}\%$
- 40%
- $66\frac{2}{3}\%$
- 72%

Explanation

We can write a weighted average for the amount of parsley in the final mixture. In general, where a weighted average is possible, it will be the fastest route to solving a question. We can call X the proportion of mixture A.

$$X(0.60) + (1 - X)(0.25) = 0.35$$

Thinking of this as an average, we can get a sense of how X and $1 - X$ compare. 0.60 is 0.25 away from the final value, whereas 0.25 is only 0.10 away from the final value. For the second term to have the influence, it has, $1 - X$ must be somewhere around 2.5 times the value of X. So X is a pretty modest percentage. Even (B) looks too big; the odds are strong that (A) is the answer. We can confirm:

$$(0.28)(0.60) + (0.72)(0.25) = 0.35$$

$$0.168 + 0.18 = 0.35$$

This statement is not quite correct, but it's quite close; indeed, the question says "approximately."

The correct answer is (A).

If $1 - \frac{1}{y} = \frac{y}{4}$, then y has how many possible values?

- None
- One
- Two
- A finite number greater than one
- An infinite number

Possible Values of Y

If $1 - \frac{1}{y} = \frac{y}{4}$, then y has how many possible values?

- None
- One
- Two
- A finite number greater than one
- An infinite number

Explanation

This question presents us with a quadratic equation in disguise, so barring something unexpected, we'll have two roots that may or may not be distinct, so the answer is probably (C) or (B).

$$1 - \frac{1}{y} = \frac{y}{4}$$

$$4y - 4 = y^2$$

$$y^2 - 4y + 4 = 0$$

$$(y - 2)(y - 2) = 0$$

There is only one possible value for y, 2.

The correct answer is (B).

A game is played with a deck of cards all numbered with either 2, 3, 5, or 7 spots. The point value of a card is its number of spots, unless it is a red card, in which case the point value of the card is 13. In one instance, ten cards are drawn from the container. If the product of the point values of the removed cards is 5,733,000, how many black 7-spot cards were drawn?

- 5
- 4
- 3
- 2
- 0

Game with Cards and Point Values

A game is played with a deck of cards all numbered with either 2, 3, 5, or 7 spots. The point value of a card is its number of spots, unless it is a red card, in which case the point value of the card is 13. In one instance, ten cards are drawn from the container. If the product of the point values of the removed cards is 5,733,000, how many black 7-spot cards were drawn?

- 5
- 4
- 3
- 2
- 0

Explanation

In this question, the colors of the cards are not truly essential. The point is that each card is worth 2, 3, 5, 7, or 13 points. Since those are all primes, and we have the product of a series of draws, we can determine exactly how many draws of each time occurred by finding the prime factorization of 5,733,000:

$$= 5733 \times 10^3$$

Since $5 + 7 + 3 + 3 = 18$ is divisible by 9, the number 5733 is divisible by 9.

$$= (9)(637) \times 10^3$$

$$= (9)(7)(91) \times 10^3$$

$$= (9)(7)(7)(13) \times (2)(2)(2)(5)(5)(5)$$

We have identified the 10 cards that were drawn. We need the number of black 7 cards, which correspond to the factors of 7. There are two, so we now know the correct answer is (D).

Another straightforward way to solve this question is to divide 5,733,000 by 7, obtaining 819,000, then to divide 819,000 by 7, obtaining 117,000, and then attempting to divide by 7 a third time and finding it doesn't go in evenly, meaning that 5,733,000 has two factors of 7.

Note that this question would be somewhat more complicated if we didn't know the number of cards that were drawn. For example, in such a case, we wouldn't know whether the factors (9)(7)(7) were generated by two black 7 cards and a black 9 card, or by 63 black 7 cards!

The correct answer is (D).

If r, s, and t are consecutive even integers and $r < s < t$, which of the following must be true?

I. $t - r = 4$

II. $(s - r)t$ is an even integer.

III. $\frac{r+s+t}{3}$ is an even integer.

- I only
- II only
- I and II only
- II and III only
- I, II, and III

Properties of Consecutive Even Integers

If r, s, and t are consecutive even integers and $r < s < t$, which of the following must be true?

I. $t - r = 4$

II. $(s - r)t$ is an even integer.

III. $\frac{r+s+t}{3}$ is an even integer.

- o I only
- o II only
- o I and II only
- o II and III only
- o I, II, and III

Explanation

In this question, the numbers r, s, and t could be 4, 6, 8, or 52, 54, 56, to pick two cases of many. We can also think of them as r, $s = r + 2$, $t = r + 4$. That observation leads us to see that Roman numeral I must be true. Answer choices (B) and (D) are out. Roman numeral II must be true, because $s - r$ is always an integer and t is even, so the factor of 2 will carry over into the product and make it even. We can evaluate Roman numeral III with numbers or algebra. It says that

$$\frac{r + r + 2 + r + 4}{3} = \text{integer}$$

$$\frac{3r + 6}{3} = \text{integer}$$

$$r + 2 = \text{integer}$$

This is true. Therefore, III must also be true. All three must be true.

The correct answer is (E).

In a courtyard, one bell rings every $\frac{1}{4}$ hour and other bell rings every $\frac{1}{5}$ hour. Both bells ring together exactly at the beginning of each hour. Which of the following gives all of the intervals that occur between any two rings of a bell, in minutes?

- 6 and 9 only
- 3, 6, and 9
- 3, 12, and 15
- 3, 6, 9, and 12
- 3, 6, 10, and 12

Minutes of Courtyard Bell

In a courtyard, one bell rings every $\frac{1}{4}$ hour and other bell rings every $\frac{1}{5}$ hour. Both bells ring together exactly at the beginning of each hour. Which of the following gives all of the intervals that occur between any two rings of a bell, in minutes?

- 6 and 9 only
- 3, 6, and 9
- 3, 12, and 15
- 3, 6, 9, and 12
- 3, 6, 10, and 12

Explanation

In this question, one bell rings every 15 minutes and the other rings every 12 minutes, and they are synchronized on the hour. So the minutes of the rings of the first bell are 0, 15, 30, 45, and 60. The minutes of the second bell's rings are 0, 12, 24, 36, 48, and 60. Combining them, the rings happen at

0, 12, 15, 24, 30, 36, 45, 48, 60

Comparing our list with the answer choices: there are intervals of 3, so (A) is out. There are no intervals of 15, so (C) is out. There are intervals of 12, so (B) is out. We are left with (D) and (E). From 36 to 45 is 9 minutes.

The correct answer is (D).

If k is a positive integer, then $k(k + 1)(k + 3)$ is

- even only when k is even
- even only when k is odd
- odd whenever k is odd
- divisible by 3 only when k is odd
- divisible by 4 whenever k is odd

Even and Odd Properties of Algebraic Expression

If k is a positive integer, then $k(k+1)(k+3)$ is

- even only when k is even
- even only when k is odd
- odd whenever k is odd
- divisible by 3 only when k is odd
- divisible by 4 whenever k is odd

Explanation

In this question, we can solve this question with odd and even rules, using cases to remind ourselves of the rules or clarify confusing points. Glancing at the answer choices, part of the issue is what happens when k is even or odd. If k is even, the whole thing will be even, since it only takes one even number. Therefore, (B) is out. If k is odd, then $k+1$ will be even, and the whole thing will be even. That fact knocks out answer choices (A) and (C). (D) doesn't seem right: what if $k=6$? Then k=even and the whole thing is divisible by 3, since 6 is a factor. That leaves only (E). Indeed, if k is odd, then the other two factors are even, so the product will have at least two 2's.

The correct answer is (E).

How many circles can be constructed in the coordinate plane that have a center at (r, s), where r and s are integers, that have a radius with an integer length, and that in no portion lie outside the square region defined by $0 \leq x \leq 5$ and $0 \leq y \leq 5$?

- 16
- 20
- 21
- 24
- 25

Circles Within a Square

How many circles can be constructed in the coordinate plane that have a center at (r, s), where r and s are integers, that have a radius with an integer length, and that in no portion lie outside the square region defined by $0 \leq x \leq 5$ and $0 \leq y \leq 5$?

- 16
- 20
- 21
- 24
- 25

Explanation

In this question, we want to know the number of circles that fit inside a 5-by-5 box in the coordinate plane. We can consider the circles of different radii in turn. The smallest circles have a radius of 1. They can exist at (1, 1), or any combination of integers in the interior of this space apart from the edges. That's a total of $4 \times 4 = 16$ possible centers. When the radius is 2, there are fewer possibilities; the outer rectangle of points allowed for circles of radius 1 are removed, leaving $2 \times 2 = 4$ possibilities. No circle of radius 3 fits in the space if it is centered on integer coordinates, so we have considered all possible cases, which total $16 + 4 = 20$.

The correct answer is (B).

If $\frac{0.016 \times 10^n}{0.4 \times 10^m} = 4 \times 10^4$, then $m - n =$

- 6
- 4
- 0
- −4
- −6

Fraction of Decimals and Exponents

If $\frac{0.016 \times 10^n}{0.4 \times 10^m} = 4 \times 10^4$, then $m - n =$

- 6
- 4
- 0
- -4
- -6

Explanation

In this question, we can convert the numerator and denominator of the fraction to simpler forms.

$$\frac{0.016 \times 10^n}{0.4 \times 10^m} = 4 \times 10^4$$

$$\frac{16 \times 10^{-3} \times 10^n}{4 \times 10^{-1} \times 10^m} = 4 \times 10^4$$

$$\frac{16 \times 10^{n-3}}{4 \times 10^{m-1}} = 4 \times 10^4$$

$$\frac{10^{n-3}}{10^{m-1}} = 10^4$$

$$(n - 3) - (m - 1) = 4$$

$$n - 3 - m + 1 = 4$$

$$n - m - 2 = 4$$

$$n - m = 6$$

$$m - n = -6$$

The correct answer is (E).

The value of $3^{-2} + 3^{-4} + 3^{-6}$ is how many times the value of 3^{-5}?

- $\frac{91}{3}$
- 27
- $\frac{31}{3}$
- 3
- $\frac{1}{3}$

Multiple of an Exponent

The value of $3^{-2} + 3^{-4} + 3^{-6}$ is how many times the value of 3^{-5}?

- $\frac{91}{3}$
- 27
- $\frac{31}{3}$
- 3
- $\frac{1}{3}$

Explanation

To answer this question, we need to factor a 3^{-5} out of the expression $3^{-2} + 3^{-4} + 3^{-6}$ so that

$$3^{-5}(\text{something}) = 3^{-2} + 3^{-4} + 3^{-6}$$

The first term, to yield 3^{-2} when multiplied by 3^{-5}, must have a power of positive 3. Carrying this logic through, we get

$$3^{-5}(3^3 + 3^1 + 3^{-1}) = 3^{-2} + 3^{-4} + 3^{-6}$$

$$3^{-5}\left(27 + 3 + \frac{1}{3}\right) = 3^{-2} + 3^{-4} + 3^{-6}$$

And $27 + 3 + \frac{1}{3} = 30\frac{1}{3} = \frac{91}{3}$.

The correct answer is (A).

How many of the integers that satisfy the inequality $(y + 1)(y + 2)(y + 4) \geq 0$ are less than 4?

- 4
- 5
- 6
- 7
- 8

INTEGERS SATISFYING AN INEQUALITY

How many of the integers that satisfy the inequality $(y + 1)(y + 2)(y + 4) \geq 0$ are less than 4?

- 4
- 5
- 6
- 7
- 8

EXPLANATION

In this question, one approach would be to multiply the left side of the inequality, but that leads to messy algebra with a y cubed term. Moreover, we are talking about only 10 or so cases, judging by the answer choices. So we can start with the integer 3 and evaluate, counting down until we have enough information to determine the correct answer.

If $y = 3$, then $(y + 1)(y + 2)(y + 4) = (4)(5)(7) \geq 0$, so 3 counts.

Since we want to be positive, $y = 2$ and $y = 1$ will also count, bringing our count to 3.

If $y = 0$, we have a similar case, bringing the count to 4.

If $y = -1$, one of the factors is 0, making the whole thing 0. But that satisfies the condition ≥ 0, so $y = -1$ counts, bringing the total count to 5.

If $y = -2$, we have a zero, so that raises the count to 6.

If $y = -3$, then $(y + 1)(y + 2)(y + 4) = (-2)(-1)(1) = 2 \geq 0$, and we the product of two negative numbers and a positive number, so it counts. That brings us to 7.

Finally, $y = -4$ gives us a zero, so that's 8.

The correct answer is (E).

What's Next?

You've made it to the end of the book! Here are some next steps:

- Your purchase of this book comes with a free download, a handy short reference (plus whatever we have lately to offer digitally): the **Problem Solving Strategy Sheets**. You can get the download at www.gmatfree.com/PS-Strategy-Sheets.

- At this point, Data Sufficiency is key to preparing for the Quant section. The better you do on the Quantitative section, the more Data Sufficiency you'll see. To practice Data Sufficiency for free, join us online at www.gmatfree.com.

- A more general list of GMAT Prep resources is available on our "GMAT Prep" page online at www.gmatfree.com/gmat-prep/. This page includes links to important resources such as GMATPrep, the software from the test maker.

- If you found this book useful, we would appreciate your positive review of it on Amazon. We also welcome your questions and constructive feedback at www.gmatfree.com/contact-us/.

Good luck in your GMAT preparation and on the path to business school.

Warm regards,

Andrew Mitchell
Chief Freedom Officer
GMAT Free, LLC

>> Download the free
PS Strategy Sheets
GMATFree.com/PS-Strategy-Sheets

INDEX OF QUESTIONS

30th Digit	33
A Difference and a Total	167
A Machine's Rate of Production	169
A Painting Machine's Rate	331
A Projectile Falls Short	313
Absolute Value Inequality	35
Absolute Value on Number Line	23
Albert's Coins	257
Algebraic Divisibility by 3	171
Algebraic Equivalence	71
Algebraic Manipulation of a Median	189
Angles and Fractions of a Circle	81
Angles of a Parallelogram	121
Approaching Cars	411
Area of Irregular Shape	329
Arithmetic Sequence	247
Arithmetic with Fractions	191
Assigning Pairs	265
Average Excluding Tax	269
Average with Additional Item	55
Average with New Element	403
Beginning and End of a Season	371
Bisecting a Line	87
Bucket of Rainwater	111
Buses, Passengers, and Folders	3
Cannot Be Odd	85
Carrots and Onions Purchased	123
Change in Health Care Cost per Employee	349
Change in Sales Ratio	221
Changing an Apples-to-Oranges Ratio	201
Chris' Average Expenses	285
Circle in the Coordinate Plane	133
Circles Within a Square	449
Circular Garden and Circular Statue	339
Citizenship Survey	383
Combined Rate of Nail-Producing Machines	173
Combined Rate of Two Machines	279
Combining Inequalities	147
Combining Inequalities II	255
Commission on Sales	29

Company Satisfaction Rate	229
Comparing Car Counts at a Location	143
Comparing Exponents	217
Comparing Mean and Median	129
Comparing Medians	263
Comparing Two Averages	103
Compound Interest	165
Consecutive Odd Integers	183
Contaminated Volume in a Tank	197
Converting Units	127
Counting Nonzero Digits	343
Counting Prime Number Factors	337
Counting Zeroes	219
Custom Operation	293
Dates at a Wedding Reception	79
Day Shift and Night Shift	45
Decline in a Road	175
Decreasing with y	395
Definition: Less Than or Equal To	297
Difference in Distances over Time	95
Differing Powers and Denominators	435
Dimensions of a Window	287
Distance to the Moon	135
Distance within a Box	399
Distances in the Coordinate Plane	393
Distribution of Charitable Donation	401
Dive Into a Pool of Water	261
Divisibility by Twice a Square	303
Divisibility into Paperclip Piles	149
Divisibility of a Large Number	159
Doubling Investment	273
Driving at a Constant Rate	67
Earnings per Team and per Member	305
Earthquake Strength	195
Ed's Research Estimate	267
Eduardo's Heaviest Catches	299
Employees from England and Japan	357
Equal Rectangular Areas	11
Equation of a Line	117
Equation of Line L	413
Ernesto and His Wife's Ages	177
Estimating a Sum of Many Fractions	163
Estimating Sum of Fractions	89

Even and Odd Properties of Algebraic Expression	447
Exchanging Digits	425
Factor of a Large Product	223
Family Savings	9
Finding a Non-Factor	231
Fraction of Decimals and Exponents	451
Fraction of Many Decimals	161
Fraction Subtraction	91
Fraction with Repeating Decimals	309
Fractions of Inventory	19
Fractions, Decimals and Denominators	75
Frederique's Trip	315
Fresh Fish Average of Averages	25
Game with Cards and Point Values	441
Game with Six-Sided Die	419
Generating a Non-Integer	7
Graph of Hours Worked	61
Gross Profit per Light Bulb	179
Identification Numbers	27
Import Taxes	47
Impossible Value of k	353
Improper Fraction	277
Increasing a Percent	289
Inequalities with a Negative Fraction	239
Insect Population Growth	207
Integers Satisfying an Inequality	455
Integers Within an Inequality	101
Interior and Exterior Angles of Triangle	421
Jay's Painting Rate	69
Jenna's Children	367
John's and Janice's Age	341
Least Common Multiple	83
Lecture Hall Seats	15
Legal Service Billing	283
Linear Equation with Variable in Denominator	369
Linear Equations with Fractions	213
Livestock per Capita	275
Machines and Combined Rate	37
Maximum Divisors	215
Men and Women Assigned to Projects	105
Minutes of Courtyard Bell	445
Mixture of Spices	437

Molecules of Carbon Dioxide in a Sample	365
Monthly Customer Acquisition	225
Multiple of an Exponent	453
Needless Variable	141
Negative Exponents of Negative Fractions	359
Nested Rectangles	327
Nine Audio Recordings	381
Non-Linear Equation	423
Non-Prime Divisors of n	407
Number Line Segment	281
One-Tenth Percent	21
Operation Omega	259
Operations on Unknown Number	333
Other Solution of a Quadratic Equation	97
Overlapping Frames	237
Overlapping Sets – Questions Answered Correctly	389
People Registered to Vote	199
Percent Decrease in Value	193
Percent Increases and Decreases	63
Percent of a Number	43
Percent of x	361
Percentage to Range Estimate	295
Piles of Coins	59
Points in Coordinate Plane	51
Portions of Advanced Certification	351
Possible Absolute Values	93
Possible Answers to a Survey	307
Possible Values of y	439
Powers of Negative 1	323
Powers of Tenth	41
Prime Number and Remainder	49
Prime Number Manipulation	243
Probability of a Product	385
Probability of Coin Tosses	391
Probability of Pairs of Draws	137
Properties of Consecutive Even Integers	443
Quadratic Equation	377
Quadratic Inequality	363
Quotients of Positive and Negative Numbers	73
Radical and Power	13
Ratio of a Cylinder's Dimensions	241
Ratio of Mean to Median	209

Download the free PS Strategy Sheets at GMATFree.com/PS-Strategy-Sheets

Ratio of Profits	151
Ratio of Substances in a Solution	405
Ratio of Women to Men	233
Ratio with a Fraction	53
Ratios of Children	139
Ratios of Marbles	107
Rectangular Floor	17
Recursive Sequence	325
Remainder and Fractional Portion	185
Restaurant Reviews – Overlapping Sets	373
Retailer's Profit on Items Ordered	355
Revenue from Sweaters	181
Rotating a Square	145
Rounded Weight and Actual Weight	291
Salt Solution	335
Scanning the Pages of a Book	203
Seminar Overflow	235
Serving Size, Price and Revenue	125
Simplifying Radicals	65
Skiing Club Members…and the Whole Class	379
Slope of a Line	119
Solving by Exponent Rules	245
Solving for x in Compound Fraction	429
Spending Cash Reserves	113
Stairway of Blocks	251
Students per Class	397
Students Who Got Both Questions Correct	433
Substitution Into an Expression	415
Subtracting Compound Fractions	57
Suggestive Fraction	387
Sum of Many Odd Integers	345
Sum of Primes	5
Sum of Sit-Ups Over a Year	311
Summing Radicals	109
Surface Area of Tile Fragments	301
Symmetric Distribution	227
Tangent Circle	417
Teachers Aged 30+	211
Team Award	157
Teams Finishing Foot Race	39
Terms in a Closed-Form Sequence	375
The Diagonal of a Square	205
The Probability of a Blue Ball	347

Thermal Resistances	431
Three Posts	253
Three Product Launches	427
Time to Turn Around	155
Trapezoid and Circle	321
Triangle in the Coordinate Plane	409
Two Equations Plus One Condition	99
Two Quadratic Equations	187
Unemployed Miners	271
Unique Code System	249
Units Digit of an Exponent	317
Value of Quadratic Expression	319
Variable in a Denominator	77
Visible Stars in the Night Sky	131
Volume from Area	153
Volume of Two Boxes	31
Volumes of a Solution	115

>> Download the free **PS Strategy Sheets**

GMATFree.com/PS-Strategy-Sheets

Printed in Great Britain
by Amazon